FOUNDATIONS OF ETHICS
A Critical Reader in Moral and Social Philosophy

FOUNDATIONS OF ETHICS
A Critical Reader in Moral and Social Philosophy

F. Ochieng'-Odhiambo

University of Nairobi Press

First published 2009 by
University of Nairobi Press (UONP)
Jomo Kenyatta Memorial Library
University of Nairobi
P.O. Box 30197 – 00100 Nairobi
E-mail: nup@uonbi.ac.ke
www.uonbi.ac.ke/press

© University of Nairobi Press, 2009

The moral rights of the author have been asserted.

The University of Nairobi Press supports and promotes University of Nairobi's objectives of discovery, dissemination and preservation of knowledge, and stimulation of intellectual and cultural life by publishing works of the highest quality in association with partners in different parts of the world. In doing so, it adheres to the University's tradition of excellence, innovation and scholarship.

University of Nairobi Library CIP Data

Ochieng'-Odhiambo, F.
Foundation of ethics: a critical reader in moral and social philosophy / F. Ochieng'-Odhiambo.–Nairobi: University of Nairobi Press, 2009.
220p
1. Ethics   I. Title
BJ 1012.02

All rights reserved. Except for the quotation of fully acknowledged short passages for the purposes of criticism, review, research or teaching, no part of this publication may be reproduced, stored in any retrieval system, or transmitted in any form or means without a prior written permission from the University of Nairobi Press.

ISBN: 9966 846 00 X

Printed by
Starbright Services Ltd.
P.O. Box 66949-00200
Nairobi

Contents

Preface ix

Part 1: Basic Concepts

1. Ethical Relativism 1
2. Universality and Ethics: Supervenience 7
3. *Prima Facie* and the Resultant Moral Concepts 13
4. Restricted and Unrestricted Ethical Relativism 19
5. Two Kinds of Judgements 25
6. Ethical Relativism and Ethical Absolutism 29
   Cultural or Belief Relativism 29
   Differences in Resultant Rightness or Wrongness 29
7. Defining Ethical Terms and Criteria 35
   Two Types of Disagreement 38
   Hybrid Judgements 41

Part 2: Two Theories of Ethics

8. The Basic Teleological Principle 47
   Is the Basic Teleological Principle a (BTP) Truism? 48
   The "Subjectivity" Problem 50
9. Deontological Theories of Ethics 55
   Deontology and Teleology: The Logical Difference 58
   Epistemological Difference 59
   Right or Wrong Independent of the consequences versus Right or Wrong, No Matter What the Consequences 60
   Utilitarian Theory of Promising 63
   Human Society: With or without promises or agreements 72

10.	Theories of Punishment	77
	The Utilitarian Theory	*78*
	The Deontological Theory or Retributivism	*79*
	Utilitarianism versus Deontology	*79*
11.	Justice and the Obligation not to punish the Innocent	85
	The Dreyfus Affair	*86*
	Restricted versus Unrestricted Retributivism	*89*
	Reflections on Punishing the Innocent	*92*
	Utilitarianism, Deontology and Formalism	*96*
	Moral Views versus Moral Theories	*97*
	Formalism: Pacifism	*99*
12.	Deontology or Retributivism and the Results of Punishment	103
	Retributivism and Recidivism	*104*
	Utilitarianism and Preventive Punishment	*107*
	Deontological Theory of Punishment and Utilitarian Considerations	*112*
	A Problem for Deontology or Retributivism: Repeat Offenders	*115*
	Deontological Obligations	*117*
	Retribution, Punishment, Revenge and Retaliation or Payback Behaviour	*125*
13.	Exceptions to Moral Principles	133
	Apparent Exceptions: Additive Whole	*133*
	Genuine Exceptions: Organic Whole	*138*
	Conclusion	*148*

Part 3: Rule-Utilitarianism and The Generalisation Argument

14.	The Generalisation Argument	151
	Utilitarianism	*151*
	Deontology	*152*
	Supervenience and Universality	*160*

15. The Generalisation Argument and The Basic
    Teleological Principle 163
    An Alternative Expression of the Generalisation Argument.......... 164
    *Conditions for the Valid Application of the Generalisation
    Argument 165*
    Reformulation of the Generalisation Argument 173
    Celibacy and the Generalisation Argument 175
    'Exceptions' to the Generalisation Argument 176
    Examples of the Generalisation Argument 178
16. Rule-Utilitarianism 183
    The Rule-Utilitarian Theory of Punishment 183
    Legal System Based on Act-Utilitarian Principles 186
    Rule-utilitarianism – A Summary 192

Review Exercises **195**

Bibliography **201**

Index **205**

Preface

Ethics is generally considered the most popular branch of philosophy with abundant philosophical literature dealing with moral principles dating back to ancient Greece. Most of this literature is, however, presented in works that contain long and complicated arguments.

Foundations of Ethics: *A Critical Reader in Moral and Social Philosophy* is an introductory text meant for beginners. It presents and discusses standard ethical terms and positions in a simple and clear manner by using real life examples most of which the reader will find refreshing. It aims at stimulating and encouraging the readers to undertake better philosophical thinking about ethical questions.

The book is divided into three parts. *Part One* takes the student through an exploration of some basic moral terms, concepts, principles and views. *Part Two* is devoted to two ethical theories: teleology and deontology while *Part Three* enunciates and discusses rule-utilitarianism, a third ethical theory. Some ethical terms and issues though, seemingly simple, are often controversial even among philosophers. In order to minimize the controversy, one of the ways is to explain and discuss the issues with logical rigour and force. This text has been written in that vein. The style and simplicity of expression that run throughout the text, coupled with the examples provided should make it suitable to undergraduate students of philosophy in general and those of ethics in particular. Students of law, sociology, political science, religious studies and the general public should find it a useful companion because of its multi-disciplinary approach. A review exercise is included at the end of the text to assist the student test his/her understanding of the concepts and issues discussed.

Many people have made the writing and publication of this text possible. I wish to thank Dr. Eugene Valberg for initiating and sustaining my interest in the art and science of clear thinking during my undergraduate and postgraduate studies in philosophy at the

University of Nairobi. My thanks also go to Prof. D. A. Masolo and to the late Prof. H. Odera Oruka. The two played an instrumental role in my academic development. I am also indebted to Prof. Robert Murungi of Kenyatta University for his incisive comments after reading the original manuscript I submitted for publication. I found his criticisms to be constructive and quite invaluable. My gratitude must also be extended to the School of Graduate Studies and Research, University of the West Indies, Cave Hill Campus for financial support. I wish to thank the University of Nairobi Press staff, especially Ms. Pauline W. Mahugu, for the commendable and professional manner in which they handled the publication process of the text. I cannot forget to thank my wife, Betty Ochieng', and the children, for they created the conducive atmosphere at home which enabled me to struggle through the manuscript to the end. Finally, I wish to describe this text as 'a homage to my brother,' the late John Owino Odhiambo to whom it is dedicated.

F. Ochieng'-Odhiambo
April, 2009

Part 1
Basic Concepts

1

Ethical Relativism

Ethical relativism asserts that what is right or wrong in one place or at one time needs not be wrong at another time or another place. It asserts the possibility of a difference between what is right or wrong at one time or place as compared to another. Strictly speaking, all that is required to prove ethical relativism is the mere possibility of differences in moral perceptions. In ancient philosophical works, ethical relativism is noticeable in Aristotle's *Nicomachean Ethics* where it is asserted that "fire burns both in Hellas and in Persia, but men's ideas of right and wrong vary from place to place."

The direct logical opposite of ethical relativism is *ethical absolutism*. Whereas ethical relativism asserts the possibility of moral differences, ethical absolutism denies it and asserts that, if something is wrong in one place it cannot be right elsewhere, that is, what is wrong in one place must be wrong everywhere else. Absolutism says that if incest for example, is wrong in one place, it will be wrong everywhere else and that if it is wrong in one place it must be wrong everywhere. As will be shown later, it is not clear what a statement like "incest is wrong everywhere" would mean.

The first important point in ethical relativism and ethical absolutism is that they involve the modal concepts of necessity and possibility.

It is easy to demonstrate the argument surrounding ethical relativism by using the example of moral standards. Moral standards differ from one time or place to another; but what exactly does it mean to say, "Moral standards differ?"

(1) Abortion is wrong in Saudi Arabia or Italy but not in Japan or the U.S.A. (2) The killing of twins was at one time right in Nigeria but at present it is not.

On these two examples, there are two crucial questions to ask.

(1) What exactly does it mean when one says that abortion is wrong in Saudi Arabia but not in Japan? And (2) what reasons does one have for saying that it is wrong in that one place and not in the other?

A careful examination will show that the only reason is that abortion is an act that is considered morally wrong in Saudi Arabia and not morally wrong in Japan. These statements are about what people believe in. They are psychological, sociological or anthropological statements, which have nothing to do with the actual rightness or wrongness of abortion; just like a statement: "at one time, everyone believed that the earth was flat" would have very little to do with the actual shape of the earth. It has more to do with people's beliefs about the shape of the earth. In order to determine the truth or falsity of the statement "at one time people believed the earth to be flat" we would have to undertake historical, psychological or anthropological research. But in order to determine the truth or falsity of the statement "the earth is flat" or "at one time the earth was flat," what people believe or believed about its shape is quite irrelevant. To determine whether or not it is flat, we would have to make certain physical observations.

Similarly, to determine the truth of the statement "people in a certain culture at a certain time, believed something to be right or wrong or engaged in particular such practices" we would have to undertake empirical research of a basically sociological or anthropological nature. Once we have the data and can show that at one time people in Nigeria did in fact consider the killing of twins to be right, then that would settle the matter of what their moral beliefs were then. However, it does not settle the matter of whether what they did was right or wrong.

If the statement, "people's moral beliefs differ from one time or place to another," were true, some might think that that would be sufficient proof for ethical relativism. But if understood in this way, it does not prove, or even constitute any evidence for ethical relativism because ethical relativism is not a psychological, sociological or anthropological doctrine, but an ethical and moral doctrine. Primarily, ethical relativism does not assert that what is considered or believed to be wrong in one place may not possibly be considered wrong in another, but rather that what is wrong in one place may not be wrong in another.

Let us consider the following principles:

> Whatever is considered wrong in one place by certain persons is therefore wrong.

Or an even stronger principle, that:

> To say that X is wrong is to say that X is considered wrong.

In other words,

> (A) X is wrong = (B) X is considered wrong.

The fact that (A) is not equivalent to (B) can be seen in various ways. One, (A) is a moral type statement (if for example, X is filled in with something like 'abortion'), whereas (B) is a statement about what the case is. Thus, while (B) can, in principle, be definitely settled by appealing to empirical (psychological, sociological, anthropological) fact, (A) clearly cannot be. That is, one cannot, in any obvious way, settle the question of whether abortion is right or wrong just by appealing to any empirical facts.

Two, while (B) is clearly a contingent proposition, (A) is apparently necessary. That is, even if it is true that, "most Saudis consider abortion to be wrong," the fact that they do consider it to be so, is clearly contingent. If abortion is wrong now, it would be *prima facie* absurd to say "I know it is wrong now, but it might not be wrong in a few weeks or a few years time." Thus, moral statements are analogous to the fact that a minimum of three sides is required to make a polygon. It would be absurd to say, "I know that three sides are required to make a polygon now, but tomorrow we might be able to make one with only two sides." On the other hand, it would be less absurd to say, "I know that most Saudis today would say that abortion is wrong, but they might not say so tomorrow."

The impossibility of identifying the statement: "X is wrong" with "X is considered wrong" can be shown by the mere fact that attempting to do so leads to a vicious infinite regress.

For if the theory about what "X is wrong" were correct, we would never say what it is that people believe when they assume that abortion is wrong. Whenever we come to the phrase "abortion is wrong," we would have to substitute it with "most people believe abortion is wrong." This means that we would have to substitute it endlessly, thus getting a vicious infinite regress.

It can also be pointed out that if we accepted the view that, "if most people consider something to be wrong then it is wrong," it would then be impossible for a person to ever disagree with the majority.

The view that the majority's opinion is automatically right is absurd on logical grounds. The idea of a majority implies a minority. But if this view was taken seriously, there would be no minority, at least on moral questions. As soon as 51 per cent of a people believe that something is wrong, it would *ipso facto* be wrong and as soon as anyone in the remaining 49 per cent knew this, they would be forced, on logical grounds, to agree. The knowledge of persons in the minority that they are in the minority would force them to change their views. Anyone who would become aware that he is in the minority would automatically move over to the majority. That is, however, absurd. Numbers never determine rightness or wrongness of ethical statements.

The idea that for something to be wrong, it must be considered wrong is absurd and can be rejected. Yet, ethical relativism often rests on precisely this principle; that what is considered wrong in one place differs from what is considered wrong in another place.

Consider the following:

> What is considered wrong by some persons is wrong for them or from their point of view or wrong according to them; this is modified or restricted ethical relativism.

The question to ask here is not, whether this view is correct or not, but "what it means to say that something is wrong from one's point of view?" What does it mean, for example, to say that abortion is wrong according to Italians? By "according to them" we apparently mean "according to their belief." Hence, to say that abortion is wrong "according to Italians" means that it is wrong "according to the beliefs of most Italians." Consequently, our statement of modified or restricted ethical relativism becomes something like "If most Italians think that abortion is wrong, then it is wrong according to them, that is, it is wrong according to their beliefs, or rather, they believe it is wrong." This is a trivial tautology and is of no philosophical interest. But it is true that if most Italians think that abortion is wrong then they will necessarily think or believe that this belief of theirs is true. This is one of the two basic principles of belief:

> P1: Whatever a person believes, he necessarily believes it is true.

The other basic principle of belief is that:

> P2: The fact that someone believes something, it never follows it is true.

For example, if Nigerians believe that the killing of twins is right, they will think that this belief is true. In the second principle of belief (P2), the mere fact of thinking it is right, in no way makes it right. It should be noted also that based on P1, if we believe that our moral beliefs are true, it follows that any belief contrary to our own is false.

What has been said so far concerns one argument in support of ethical relativism and it has been confirmed that this argument is incorrect. This argument asserts that what is considered wrong in one place may not be considered wrong in another place, and that what is wrong in one place may not be wrong in another place. The fact that this argument is not valid does not mean ethical relativism is false, but that one line of reasoning, which is the basis for it, is incorrect. The fact that an argument is invalid does not mean that the conclusion is false; but only that the argument does not give it any support.

In order to understand ethical relativism fully, one has to understand the notion of the universality of moral judgements. This in turn requires that one comes to grips with the fact that moral concepts are *higher* or *second order* concepts, or what would be referred to as *supervenient* discussed in the next chapter.

2

Universality and Ethics: Supervenience

Suppose someone says that there are two cars that are identical in all respects except for their colour–one is green and the other is blue. There would not arise any problems in understanding what he/she means. Indeed, there is nothing wrong with that statement, since two things can clearly be alike in all respects except for their colour. That might seem to be true of any property.

But can one say that two things, whatever they are, are alike in all respects except that one is good and the other is not good? Can two buildings, for example, be alike in all respects except that one is good and the other is not? If these questions do not make sense to you, why don't they?

Common sense holds that it is not possible for two things (cars, buildings, paintings) to be alike in all respects except that one is good and the other bad. This is unlike cases where it is possible for two things to be alike in all respects except that one is one colour and the other another colour. Two things cannot be alike in all other respects except that one is good and the other is not because *goodness*, whether one is referring to moral or non-moral goodness, is what is called a supervenient or higher or second order property.

So, it would be absurd to say that two paintings are alike in all other respects except that one is good and the other bad. If G is a good painting, it must be so by virtue of some of its other (first order) properties; if B is a bad painting, it must be so by virtue of lacking some of G's favourable characteristics or having some bad-making characteristics or both. If all of B's properties were identical with

G's, then if G were a good painting, then B would necessarily have to be equally good. The only way G can possibly be good while B is bad is if they differ in some other respects besides their goodness.

If C is a good car by virtue of its first order properties (dependable, economical, etc.), it then follows that any other car that has the same first order properties will have to be equally good. It would make no sense to say that C was good by virtue of properties P, Q and R, and yet D, having exactly the same properties, was not good. If C is good by virtue of having properties P, Q and R, then car D, and any other car must be equally good if it has the same properties. That explains why it is absurd to say that two things are alike in all respects except that one is good and the other is not.

Statements about higher order or supervenient properties are intrinsically universal. Whenever one says that X is good since 'good' is a supervenient property, X must be good by virtue of its other properties; and if X is good by virtue of these other properties, it follows that any other object that has the same properties as X must be equally good. If not, what reason could there be for saying that X was good by virtue of its other properties? One cannot intelligibly say that X is good by virtue of P, Q and R without pointing out that anything else that has P, Q, and R will be equally good.

Thus, to make a judgement about the goodness of a thing is necessarily making a judgement about an infinite class of objects, that is, any other objects which have those characteristics by virtue of which it is said to be good or its good characteristics.

Hence, ethical or moral judgements are universal. And moral concepts (good, bad, right, wrong, ought, ought not, etc.), are all higher order or supervenient properties. To say that some action is right or wrong is to say that it is right or wrong by virtue of some feature(s) or characteristic(s) of that action.

Basically, this is what is meant by universality of moral judgements or propositions. It is a feature of the propositions themselves, and it is in no way dependent on our knowing or saying that any particular moral proposition is true or false. Thus, consider the statement "inter-racial marriage is bad." One may regard this as false or may not know whether it is true or false, yet he can say with complete certainty that it is universal. It means that if any action has the characteristic of an inter-racial marriage, it is bad and whether this statement is true or false, it is so of any phenomenon having this characteristic. That is why one can say that the feature of being universal is a property belonging to the proposition or statement itself, irrespective of its truth or falsity.

There are many supervenient properties besides moral ones e.g. qualified, interesting, important, and funny. It is also important to consider whether certain other properties, such as *intelligence* are supervenient, and if not, why? We must also distinguish between: *(1) quality-making characteristics, (2) quality-defining characteristics, (3) quality-causing characteristics* and, *(4) quality-indicating characteristics.*

Let us expand these distinctions further: - (1) What *makes* someone to be regarded as strong could be because he is capable of lifting weights of up to 100 kilogrammes. Here the lifting of weights up to 100 kilogrammes is taken to be the criterion of being strong–its *quality-making characteristic.* (2) In another sense, lifting of weights up to 100 kilogrammes could not be seen as a criterion or standard for strong, but as what it *means* to say that someone is strong, it could be seen as the definition of strong–its *quality defining-characteristic.* (3) In yet another sense, what may make one strong is the fact that he lifts weights of up to 100 kilogrammes everyday. Here lifting of weights is neither the criterion nor meaning of strong but what *causes* one to be strong, it is the *quality-causing* characteristic. (4) We may also say that someone is strong basing our argument on the fact that we see bulging muscles beneath one's wears/cloth. This would not be the criterion, meaning, or cause of being strong. It would merely be an indication that one is strong, which is a *quality-indicating* characteristic. Each of these is distinct from the way in which someone's honesty is viewed. Honesty is neither the meaning of one being good, nor is it a cause of one's being good. It is also not an indication that one is good.

Most concepts do not have all the four kinds of characteristics. 'Intelligence', for example, has quality-defining characteristics (one can regularly perform certain tasks accurately and efficiently), quality-causing characteristics (one's education or one's genes), as well as quality-indicating characteristics (that one got a first class honours degree). But it is not clear as whether it has intelligence-making characteristics, i.e. criteria for intelligence–things that make one intelligent in the same way that things 'make' one a good or a bad person.

Similarly, one may be able to make all four distinctions with respect to moral concepts. One can distinguish between what *makes* someone a good person, e.g., honesty, from what it *means* to say that one is good (though some moral philosophers, G. E. Moore in particular, hold that 'good' cannot be defined). These two are different from what *causes* one to be good and from what is a mere *indicator* that one is good.

Another way of expressing the universal character of moral propositions is to state that time and place are irrelevant in moral judgements. If X is wrong, it will be so by virtue of certain properties (P, Q and R), so that anything having these properties will be equally wrong. Two things that cannot be relevant to the rightness or wrongness of a thing are time and place. If I say that capital punishment is wrong because it involves deliberately taking away human life, it would be absurd of someone to add "Taking a human life may not be wrong tomorrow or it may not be wrong them."

In determining whether an action is right or wrong, one has to determine what the morally relevant characteristics are. The two things that can never be relevant are the time the action occurred and the place where it occurred. At a different time and place, conditions may be different and these other conditions may be morally relevant. Thus, one's lying to somebody else today may be wrong because of the circumstances that exist today. But at another time and/or place, circumstances may be different in some morally relevant way such that lying to somebody may not be wrong, e.g. if one had to lie in order to save someone's life. What is relevant is not just the difference in time or place *per se*, but rather the different circumstances that are in existence.

The above argument has a bearing on ethical relativism, because ethical relativism asserts precisely that *what is right or wrong at one time or place may not be wrong at another time or place*. However, taken at its face value, such a view is absurd and incoherent because it amounts to the assertion that time and place are morally relevant. It would, for example, be held that even though abortion is wrong in one place by virtue of having features P, Q and R, the very same action might not be wrong in another place. This would be for no other reason other than it would be happening in another place. This is self-evidently absurd. If there is some other difference between the act that occurs at one time or place and the one at another, which is by virtue of its being wrong in one place and not in the other, then that is another matter, but neither will it be an example of ethical relativism.

If one says that abortion is wrong in Saudi Arabia but not wrong in Japan because in the latter it is needed for population control, then questions of truth or falsity aside, this would at least be logically intelligible, but it would not be an instance of ethical relativism for the person would be saying that abortion is wrong under certain conditions in Saudi Arabia, while under other conditions, as in Japan, it is not wrong. Each of these different statements–that abortion under condition C_1 is wrong, but under conditions C_2 is right–would be universally true, such that anything having the characteristics in C_1 would be wrong anywhere and anytime. Similarly, anything having the characteristics in C_2 would be right at any place and time.

3

Prima Facie and the Resultant Moral Concepts

The discussions in the just concluded chapters lead us to a very important distinction in ethics between *prima facie* and the resultant moral concepts. Suppose someone came up with the following observation in a conversation:

> Do you mean to say that, if something is wrong it must always be wrong, so that, if it is wrong to break a promise it must always, anywhere, and anytime be wrong to break a promise? Certainly that cannot be true. Suppose I borrow Kshs 1,000 from you and promise to pay it back at exactly noon on the first day of the following month since you tell me you will need it just that time. Suppose further, that as I am bringing the money, I come across a victim of a road accident, who badly needs my help. If I stop to help this person, I will not be able to keep my promise. But it might be that the right thing for me to do in these circumstances would be to help the injured person, in which case, it would be right for me to break my promise to you. In other words, it would not be wrong for me to break my promise to you, since by helping this person I will be doing the right thing–despite the fact that it involves breaking my promise to you. This then means that, there are cases where it is not wrong to break a promise. So, how can you say that if something is wrong it is wrong, everywhere and at all times? The example given is a very simple scenario where breaking a promise is not wrong.

It is important that we give a clear and correct answer to the above objection, because it borders not only on ethical relativism but also on utilitarianism as well. The answer lies in distinguishing between particular acts of breaking or keeping promises and the characteristic of breaking or keeping them. The feature or property of breaking a promise is always a *prima facie* wrong. That is, this aspect or feature of an act–which can be of an infinite number of possible actions–is in itself wrong. And the fact that any particular action involves or is an act of breaking of a promise is always a moral reason for not doing it though this reason can be outweighed by other reasons for doing the opposite. Hence, any action that involves the breaking of a promise constitutes the wrong characteristic of that action.

However, to say that an action is intrinsically wrong, that it has something wrong within it, or has one wrong characteristic does not mean that it is resultantly wrong. Saying an act is resultantly wrong means that the reasons for failing to do it outweigh the reasons *for* doing it. The fact that an act is the breaking of a promise may not be the only feature of the act that is morally relevant as in the foregoing scenario.

The breaking of a promise in this case is still *prima facie* wrong and one still has a *prima facie* obligation to keep the promise. It is only that this *prima facie* obligation is outweighed by another stronger opposite *prima facie* obligation. Thus, it would be ambiguous for anyone to say that it is always wrong to break a promise. If it means (1) that it is always *prima facie* wrong, i.e. that doing X, is always a moral reason for not doing X, then it may be true for it could be that, it is always *prima facie* wrong to break a promise. For if the fact that breaking a promise is a reason for not doing something, then it will always be and remain such a reason.

However, if the above statement is understood to mean (2) that any action which results in the breaking of a promise is always resultantly wrong, then the statement is always certainly not true. In actual fact, the statement "it is always resultantly wrong to break a promise" can be shown to be inherently irrational if not contradictory. It tends to mean that any action which involves the breaking of a promise is wrong, everything considered, and that one can say this on the basis of only one feature. That sounds contradictory because one would be saying that something is wrong based explicitly on only one consideration and not on the grounds *everything considered*.

To say that one act of promise-breaking is every*thing considered wrong* while another is *not* everything considered wrong, does not involve any kind of ethical relativism. What is wrong in one case and not wrong in the other is not the breaking of a promise itself. In fact, the breaking of a promise itself is *prima facie* wrong in both cases. What is wrong in one case and not wrong in the other is the action taken as a whole, which is quite different. If I am on my way returning the borrowed money as promised, and I am tempted to buy something with this money, it would be resultantly wrong for me to break the promise just because I want to buy that thing. If I had promised to return the money at some appointed time, then that by itself creates a strong *prima facie* obligation to do so. Given that I do not have a strong reason for not keeping my promise, I therefore, have a resultant obligation to repay it. In this case, I ought, everything considered, to have returned it as promised.

One should by now be able to easily deal with the following purported example of ethical relativism: Suppose someone says that while it would be wrong in Kenya for someone to abandon his parents to starvation, for the Eskimos who live near the North Pole, it would not be wrong to do so. The reason given would be that the Eskimos live a marginal existence of fishing and hunting, always moving from place to place. As a result, when someone becomes too old to take care of himself/herself, that person becomes an intolerable burden to the group and so must be left behind, even though that means that person is left to freeze or starve to death. So, it can be said that what is wrong in one place is right in another place.

It is to be noted that this Eskimos case differs from the one discussed in Chapter One, whereby something considered wrong in one place, is not necessarily considered so in another. In this particular case, it is a matter of one thing actually being wrong in one place and being right in another. So, we cannot deal with this case in the same way we did with the previous example.

What is wrong in one culture and right in another is not the same thing. What is wrong in Kenya is leaving one's parents to die of starvation when one is able to take care of them without such an act having disastrous consequences for the group. What is not wrong in Eskimoland is leaving one's parents to die of starvation because failure to do so would lead to everyone perishing. We could still say that leaving someone to die of starvation is *prima facie* wrong; it is wrong in Kenya and it is wrong in Eskimoland. In Eskimoland, given their circumstances, such actions are not, everything considered, on balance, resultantly wrong. Its *prima facie* wrongness is alleviated by the fact that, if they could take their parents along without risking the destruction of the group, then it would be a better alternative. Given that they cannot do that, then leaving them to starve is a better alternative than the whole group perishing.

Thus, the above example, (which at first impression seems to be an example of ethical relativism,) is in fact not one at all. There are two ethical or moral principles involved in the example: (1) That it is a *prima facie* wrong to leave someone to die of starvation. (2) That it is a *prima facie* wrong to do anything that would lead to the destruction of all members of the group. Both these principles are true at all times and in all places, (if they are true at all) and if they are false, then they are false everywhere and at all times. Thus, should conditions change so that, for example, people in Kenya could not take care of their parents without the rest of the family perishing, then it would not be wrong, everything considered, to leave them to starve. In other words, if the conditions in Kenya were to become what they are in Eskimoland, then what is now right in Eskimoland would be right in Kenya, as well.

Here is a simple example to illustrate the same logical point. We can say that human pain and suffering is bad. Suppose someone argues: "How about the pain you might experience in having a tooth extracted in order to avoid losing all your teeth; it would be painful, but would it be bad?" One can respond by saying that the pain in and of itself would be bad. What would not be bad would be the action taken as a whole that is, having your tooth extracted so that you will not lose the rest. This involves pain and yet it is good, that is, everything considered, good. However, the pain involved here is still bad; its badness is outweighed by the goodness of saving your other teeth. Its badness is made lighter by the fact that if the dentist can extract the tooth without causing the pain, it would be better still.

To summarise this discussion *vis-à-vis* ethical relativism, we can assert that there are two kinds of cases that can be presented as instances of ethical relativism:

(1) The first consists of examples where the moral beliefs of one society differ from the moral beliefs of another. Such examples, which could be called instances of cultural or belief relativism, do not constitute cases of ethical relativism. We could only get ethical relativism from such examples if we either (a) equated "X is wrong" with 'X is considered wrong," or (b) assumed some principle like "whatever people think is wrong is therefore wrong." We have also seen that neither of these is acceptable.

(2) The second case consists of examples where something is resultantly wrong in one culture but not in another culture. In such cases, it is not one and the same thing that is wrong and not wrong, but rather the action taken as a whole. It is still true that if the conditions were the same, an action that would be resultantly right in one place would be right anywhere and at anytime.

Underlying all this is the fact that moral propositions are necessarily universal; moral properties are supervenient, that is, higher order properties; and time and place are, in and of themselves, morally irrelevant.

4

Restricted and Unrestricted Ethical Relativism

Ethical relativism can take two different forms. These are *restricted* and *unrestricted* ethical relativism. Unrestricted ethical relativism states that:

> Whatever most people in any society believe to be right or wrong is right or wrong.

Having understood that such a view is unacceptable, we are likely to attempt to defend a modified or restricted form of relativism. Restricted ethical relativism states that:

> Whatever most people in any given society believe is right or wrong is right or wrong for them though perhaps not for everyone.

It is worth noting that these two forms of ethical relativism are merely instances of a more general form of relativism, epistemological relativism. The first one is an instance of unrestricted general relativism:

> Whatever one or more person(s) believe is true, is true.

And the second one is that of restricted general relativism:

> Whatever one or more person(s) believe is true, is true for that person or for them.

Ethical relativism, whether restricted or unrestricted, refers to the above two ideas applied to ethical or moral beliefs. It should also be noted that we could easily express ethical relativism as applying to individuals as well as to (most) people in a society. Thus, unrestricted ethical relativism could be expressed as:

> Whatever a person believes is right or wrong is right or wrong.

And restricted ethical relativism as:

> Whatever a person believes is right or wrong is right or wrong for that person.

We have already explained that what is wrong with unrestricted relativism is that it contradicts the second principle or belief, which says:

> The fact that someone believes something, it never follows that the belief is true.

The contradiction of this principle of belief leads to total incoherence, because it allows any and all beliefs to be true–including their contradictions. Thus, if you believe that unrestricted general relativism is true, it would mean that what you believe must be correct since whatever a person believes to be true, is true. On the other hand, if I believe that unrestricted general relativism is false and that your view is not correct, then my belief must also be true. Hence, unrestricted general relativism must be false and your view is not correct. We therefore have an inconsistent where unrestricted general relativism is both correct and not correct.

This would mean that one's 'easy gains' as a result of advocating unrestricted general relativism–that any and all of our beliefs automatically become true–is precisely balanced by equally 'easy losses'.

Based on this view, everything turns out to be true, which is really the same as saying that *nothing is true*. You could say that this view–which amounts to the denial of the second principle of belief– negates the very distinction between truth and falsity. A person who adopts this extreme view would in effect be abandoning all reasoning and there would be no point therefore in even arguing or discussing anything with that person since all argument or reasoning depends on the principle of contradiction, that:

> One and the same proposition or belief cannot be true and false.

Argument and proof have no point if we abandon the principle of contradiction, for if one was to prove to such a person, for example, that abortion is wrong, he could simply say "You are right, abortion is wrong but because I believe it is not wrong, it is also not wrong." If you were to respond, "But how can something be wrong and right at the same time?" he might answer, "You are right, it can't be; but since I believe that it can be, it can also be." If a proposition and its contradiction can both be true, then nothing is true or false.

It is because of the incoherence of unrestricted relativism that one naturally finds an alternative in restricted relativism. "Well, if it cannot be the case that because I believe that something is true, it therefore is true; at least it can be true for me." This has already been discussed at one level, where we said that the only intelligible meaning that can be given to the notion that something is true for a person is that it is "true according to that person's belief." That in turn, means that the person believes it.

In effect then, restricted relativism, whether ethical or general, is just another way of asserting the first principle of belief, which says *whatever one believes is true* it is actually true. If you believe abortion is wrong, then according to restricted ethical relativism, it follows that, that belief is true for you. However, we also know that on the basis of the second principle of belief, the fact that you or someone else holds a belief does not and cannot make it true. It merely makes it "true for you," that is, it guarantees your belief, *that it is true.*

As we have already seen, restricted ethical relativism asserts that when most people believe that X is wrong, then at least X is wrong for them, though perhaps not wrong for everyone else. We apparently have two ideas here, namely, "wrong for so and so" and "wrong for everyone."

For "wrong for everyone" we get the first version of restricted ethical relativism which states:

> If most people believe that X is wrong for everyone, then X is wrong for them, though perhaps not wrong for everyone.

If, on the other hand, we understand this first 'wrong' to mean "wrong for them", we get the second version of restricted ethical relativism which states:

> If most people believe X is wrong for them, then X is wrong for them, though perhaps not wrong for everyone.

Some ethnic groups for example, believe that it is right to circumcise girls since it makes them graduate into adulthood. They believe Circumcision of Girls (COG) is right. So, if we accept the first version of restricted ethical relativism, we could make the following statements:

(1) If all members of ethnic group Y believe that COG is right for everyone, then it is right for them though perhaps it is not right for everyone.

(2) If we believe that COG is wrong for everyone, it is wrong for us, though perhaps it is not wrong for everyone.

Let us examine the two statements carefully, beginning with the first one. When we say that COG "may not be right for everyone," we are in effect saying that the belief of ethnic group may not be true. So we are saying, as 'outsiders', that if they believe that COG is right for everyone, then a different view that it is right for them, may be true. In spite of this fact, their actual belief may just as well be false or true. Specifically, it will be false if anyone else believes that COG is wrong for everyone.

Looking at (1), which is a third person expression of the first version of restricted ethical relativism as applied to members of ethnic group Y's belief that COG is right for everyone, is there anything paradoxical about it? Does it involve any kind of contradiction or absurdity? Looking at it as someone else's beliefs and not our own beliefs, we can say that though they believe that COG is right for everyone, this belief may not be false, and all that may be true is the weaker proposition that COG is right for them. No contradiction is therefore involved.

There is, however, a contradiction in (2). This is because in the third person statement (1), we could say, as outsiders of ethnic group Y "Yes, they think COG is wrong for everyone and though that makes it wrong for them, it does not make it wrong for everyone. Their belief that COG is wrong for everyone need not be true," we cannot say the same thing of ourselves, as we are attempting to do in (2). For we are saying in (2), first, that we believe that COG is wrong for everyone and though this makes it wrong for us, it may not be wrong for everyone. If we believe and are certain that COG is wrong for everyone, we cannot turn around and say that it may not be wrong for everyone. Hence, the contradiction within (2) could be expressed as follows:

> Although we are certain that COG is wrong for everyone, it may not be wrong for everyone, so that in fact we are not certain that it is wrong for everyone.

All of this relates very closely to the first principle of belief which forces us to recognise that if we believe in something, then we must say that this belief is true. We cannot say that something is true and assert anything else which implies that it is, or may, not be true.

To summarise this discussion of the first version of restricted ethical relativism, we note that it involves a contradiction, as illustrated by the examples, expressed in (1) and (2). This contradiction can be brought out in two ways. First, it is brought out by the fact that (1) entails that COG is not wrong for members of ethnic group Y. While (2) implies that COG is wrong for members of ethnic group Y because it asserts our belief that it is wrong for everyone. Secondly, the contradiction is brought out within (2), the first part of which says that we believe COG is wrong for everyone, while the last part says that we do not believe it is wrong for everyone.

If the first version of restricted ethical relativism involves a contradiction, what about the second version:

> If most or all people believe that X is wrong for them, then it is wrong for them.

The question to examine with regard to the second version of restricted ethical relativism has to do with its basis. What would be the basis of saying that if people believe that something is wrong for them *then it is wrong for them?* It would seem that the only basis for asserting this would be the idea that whatever people believe is true, is true. That amounts to the unrestricted general relativism. When applied to ethics, unrestricted ethical relativism asserts that:

> Whatever people believe is right or wrong, is right or wrong.

However, we have already noted that unrestricted relativism, whether ethical or general, results in complete absurdity, since it contradicts the second principle of belief. It is therefore, unacceptable.

5

Two Kinds of Judgements

In the discussion of supervenience and universality, it was stated that whenever a person makes a moral or value judgement, there must always be two sets of facts or judgements involved. Moral or value judgements such as "This chalk is not good" or "That is a good car" or "Sandra is a good person" or "What you did was wrong" or "The student strike was wrong or not wrong," all involve two kinds of facts. First, the empirical judgement that the particular object in question has certain first order properties, and second, that these first order properties make the object in question good or bad, right or wrong.

The first set of judgement has the following characteristics:

- First, they are particular; they are about that one thing and nothing else.

- Second, they are *a posteriori*; we can know that the thing has these first order properties only on the basis of observation or experience.

- Thirdly, they are something about which we cannot, in principle, be certain precisely because the situation could be the other way round.

In the 18th century, a Scottish philosopher David Hume, in his book, *Inquiry Concerning Human Understanding,* made a distinction regarding the question of truth. He distinguished between analytic, *a priori* and necessary truths on the one hand, and synthetic, *a posteriori* and contingent truths on the other.

Following Hume's distinction, the second set of judgements, unlike the first set, has precisely the opposite characteristics: they are universal; are necessary; and are *a priori*. Finally, though we can know what these characteristics are, we might never be certain that they are contained in some particular act. For example, though we can say that honesty makes a person good we might not be certain that some particular person is honest.

So, when I say "this chalk is not good," what is involved in this statement? There must be something about this piece of chalk which makes me say it is bad. The chalk has certain first order properties, which makes it bad. These are its bad-making characteristics e.g. the chalk is dusty (D) and short-lasting (S). So the first fact, which has to do with particularity, contingency and *a posteriori*; is that this piece of chalk (C1), has certain first order properties such as D and S:

(1) C1 has properties D and S.

The second judgement is the universal, necessary and *a priori* judgement that D and S make a piece of chalk bad, which we can write as:

(2) D and S lead to badness in chalk.

(2) is not about this or any other particular piece of chalk. It is about all pieces of chalk in the sense that it applies to any and all pieces of chalk.

The question to carefully examine is: Which of these two sets of judgements or facts, represented by (1) and (2) constitute value judgements or facts? Which of these sets of facts are such that they constitute knowledge of value?

This is strictly analogous to a similar question we could ask about moral facts or judgements. The judgement "Sandra is a good person," involves the same sets of facts or judgements, for if Sandra is to be judged a good person, there must be something(s) about her which makes her good. These would be her good characteristics. Thus, we may say that Sandra is a good person because she is honest (H). The two statements involved here, then, would be:

(3) Sandra has the property H
   and
(4) H leads to goodness in a person.

The statement in No. 4 constitutes a moral judgement and knowledge. For if you want to give your children proper moral education, i.e. teach them right from wrong, one of the things you will want to do is to teach them that honesty is good and dishonesty bad. If, and when you succeed in doing that, you will have succeeded in imparting to them what you regard as moral knowledge. The fact that Sandra happens to be an honest person has nothing whatsoever to do with value judgement. It does not have anything to do with someone's moral education because it does not in any way, constitute a moral fact.

In the chalk example given earlier, knowing that a particular piece of chalk is dusty would be of no help at all in picking out the best chalk. If we knew that the first batch of chalk the person would see would be dusty and the second dustless, we would not need to instruct the person about the values of chalk in the first place. We would just tell the person to go and buy that kind of chalk from a particular person and a place. Knowing that some particular piece of chalk is dusty cannot possibly help the person in deciding whether or not the chalk is good.

So, the kind of knowledge we would give the person being sent out to buy the chalk, which would constitute value-judgement of chalk, is the necessary universal and *a priori* knowledge about what makes chalk good. However, for the person to choose the best chalk, he/she must also know the particular contingent and *a posteriori* facts about the chalk, i.e. which chalk is dusty and which one is dustless. The point is that this knowledge does not constitute value-knowledge of chalk and it cannot be imparted *a priori*. Only observation and experience can provide it.

6

Ethical Relativism and Ethical Absolutism

What are the general conclusions that can be drawn about ethical relativism? Two different kinds of cases, which represent an example of ethical relativism, have been considered here. These are: (1) Cultural or belief relativism and; (2) Differences in resultant rightness or wrongness.

Cultural or Belief Relativism

Cultural or belief relativism is illustrated by such examples as: "In Saudi Arabia abortion is wrong, but in Japan it is acceptable," or "In Nigeria, the killing of twins was at one time acceptable but now it is not allowed." We have seen that when such cases are examined carefully, we find that the only basis for saying that something is wrong in one place and not in another is simply that it was believed (considered) wrong in one place and not considered wrong in another. However, we have noted that this violates the second principle of belief, leads to a vicious infinite regress, as well as the possibility of contradictions.

Differences in Resultant Rightness or Wrongness

The second example of ethical relativism is illustrated by the following:
>Leaving one's parents to die of starvation would be wrong in Kenya, but would not be wrong in Eskimoland.

It is important to note that this is not merely an example of cultural or belief relativism. We are not, in this case, saying that leaving one's parents to die of starvation is considered wrong in Kenya, unlike in Eskimoland. Rather, we are saying that in Kenya it is wrong whereas in Eskimoland it is not wrong.

We have to draw a distinction between *prima facie* and resultant judgements, as well as the concepts of supervenience and universality. A *prima facie* moral judgement can be expressed as is a universal moral judgement about some characteristic–property, aspect, element, feature–which any number of particular events, acts, states of affairs or persons can have. For example, a car can be economical (E) but very unreliable (U). Unreliability (U) is a bad characteristic, while E is a good characteristic. If the badness of U outweighs the goodness of E, then the car would not be resultantly good. Even though the car is E, and therefore *prima facie* good, it is resultantly bad because U outweighs E. Nevertheless, even if some car is resultantly not good because it is U, it is still *prima facie* good if it is E.

We can, therefore, express the relationship between E and *prima facie* goodness in either of these equivalent ways:

> E implies *prima facie* goodness which can also be expressed as 'E is, a good-making characteristic' or 'E is, in and of itself, intrinsically good.'

Or

> Any car that is E is *prima facie* good, that is, it has one good thing about it.

The first illustration is explicitly about the property E while the second illustration is about any and all individual cars having that property. What it says about each and every one of these cars is that they all have one good thing about them–they are E. This fact–that each and any one of them has one good thing about them–we can express by saying that each and any one of them is *prima facie* good. Hence, saying that any and all cars that are E are *prima facie* good is in effect another way of saying that E is, in and of itself, good or is *prima facie* good.

However, just because each and every car that is E is *prima facie* good, does not mean that they are all resultantly good. For a car may be E, and therefore *prima facie* good, but so unreliable, U, that the *prima facie* badness of its U outweighs the *prima facie* goodness of its E such that everything considered–resultantly–it is not a good car and hence, one which you should not buy.

In summary, we should note that the following different judgements are involved when we make a statement like: "This is not a good car."

- E is *prima facie* good (equivalent to E is a good-making characteristic) [value judgement].
- U is *prima facie* bad [value judgement].
- This car is E (therefore *prima facie* good) [non-value judgement].
- This car is U (therefore *prima facie* bad) [non-value judgement].
- Its *prima facie* badness (U) outweighs the *prima facie* goodness (E) [value judgement].

Therefore:

- This car is, everything considered–resultantly–not good.

Value Relativism

Imagine the following scenario: Car C_1 is very economical (E) and reliable (R), but it contains parts made in the United States of America, which are not available outside North America. In North America, this would be a good car, but here in Kenya, the same car is not good. Is this an example of whether something is good in one place but not in another?

We are saying that C_1 is not a good car in Kenya everything considered. Its fuel economy and reliability are still, *prima facie* good, and hence make C_1 good. What makes the car resultantly bad in Kenya is its unreliability, and that, in turn, is due to the unavailability of parts, outside North America.

So, we have another value judgement here:

Unreliability makes a car *prima facie* bad.

The value judgement is true about any and all cars. Being unreliable makes any car, anywhere, *prima facie* bad. It is a bad car, everything considered, because it has certain bad characteristics (unreliability), which outweighs its good characteristics (E and R), and it possesses these bad characteristics accidentally in Kenya. If it had this characteristic anywhere else, it would be equally bad. It is as if someone said, "This heavy woollen coat is a good garment around the North Pole, but it is a bad garment near the Equator." There is no value relativism here. One thing is not intrinsically good because it is in one place and bad because it is in another. Rather, because of the different conditions in one place as compared to the other, the coat has different extrinsic characteristics in each place: at the North Pole, it keeps you from cold whereas around the Equator it becomes too hot. It is these different extrinsic features which make the coat resultantly good in one place and resultantly bad in the other place.

Ethical Absolutism

Ethical relativism would have to assert either one or both of the following things:

(1) It is possible that one and the same thing, one and the same property or characteristic, was both *prima facie* wrong and *prima facie* right.

(2) Some specific instance of an action could be resultantly wrong here and yet a similar action having exactly the same features as the first one be resultantly right somewhere else.

A property, being an abstract entity, is whatever it is, and has first and second order properties and cannot change. For example, if you say that honesty is in and of itself good, then you are in effect saying that the first order property of honesty has or 'produces' the second order property of goodness. If that is true of honesty, then it cannot possibly be false. The following proposition is however contingent:

Nairobi is the capital city of Kenya.

The proposition is contingent in that, though it is true, it could become false–some other city could become the capital city. What we are saying here is that a certain abstract entity–the proposition–in the above statement has the characteristic of contingency, though it is true it could be false.

Given that our statement is a contingent proposition, it cannot possibly be a necessary truth. The fact that a certain abstract entity has particular characteristics, for example, that a certain proposition is contingent it cannot possibly be something else. Whatever property an abstract entity has, it necessarily has it and cannot possibly lack that property.

Some specific instance of an action could be resultantly wrong here and yet a similar action having exactly the same features as the first one be resultantly right somewhere else. We have noted that some kind of act, for example letting one's parents die of starvation in Eskimoland could be resultantly wrong in one place, while other instances of the same act are not resultantly wrong elsewhere. This could only be possible if in one place, there are different circumstances from the first scenario such that instances of the same action have different characteristics in two different places.

Since we have assumed that there is no morally relevant difference between these two instances, the only difference can be that, one is in Kenya and the other is in Greenland. This is patently absurd for if it is the place that made a difference. It might as well just be across the room as thousands of miles away. To say "Letting one's Parents die of Starvation (LPS)" is wrong here but on that side of the room it is not" can only be understood as lacking serious reasoning.

If, on the other hand, the relativist points out some other morally relevant difference between the two cases such as LPS in Kenya and in Eskimoland; that in the extremely cold climate of Eskimoland, people beyond a certain age cannot survive the cold whether there is enough food or not, and that they are better off being left behind when others move on, then the two cases are no longer the same. In Kenya however, you have LPS without the right-making characteristics, while in Eskimoland, you have LPS where people would otherwise freeze to death.

In short, either: (1) the two cases are the same in all relevant respects in which case they must be equally right or wrong, or, (2) they are not equally right or wrong, meaning there must be some morally relevant difference by virtue of which one is resultantly wrong while the other is resultantly right.

It is this basic principle of universality, with respect to moral judgements, that ethical absolutism asserts. Since this principle seems self-evidently true, once it is understood, ethical absolutism seems to be correct. Ethical relativism, which in effect denies the universality of moral judgements, is incorrect.

7

Defining Ethical Terms and Criteria

An English philosopher, G. E. Moore, in his book, *Principia Ethica*, argues that 'good' is not analysable. He claims that 'good' is a simple concept like 'yellow', in that it cannot be 'broken up' into simpler concepts that together, will equal 'good' or 'yellow'. That is, any attempt to define or analyse it will either result in something that does not equal 'good' or it may come up with something that is in effect, the same concept as what you are trying to analyse. Thus, for example, if we try to define 'good' as "that which we ought to do," Moore would say that 'ought' here is itself an ultimate ethical or moral concept, which in this context simply means "what it would be good to do." That is, a person could only understand such a definition if he already knew what 'good' is. Therefore, it is not really a definition or analysis.

Although Moore says that 'good' cannot be defined or analysed, he does not deny that we can give its criteria, that is, say what makes something good. He has a specific theory that the only thing that is good, in and of itself, is pleasure or happiness. Nevertheless, he emphatically denies that 'good' can be defined or analysed.

It should be noted that giving a definition or analysis of a term is not the same as "giving its meaning." Moore says that we know the meaning of the word 'good,' i.e., that we have the concept 'good' and therefore know how to use the word 'good'. Indeed, he says that unless we had the concept, and hence knew what the word 'good' meant, we could possibly not ask its definition (analysis).

Similarly, though we cannot analyse the concept 'yellow' and thus cannot give a definition of the word 'yellow,' we do know what 'yellow' means, in the sense that we are aware of the concept. Unless we have the concept, we cannot possibly ask for its definition or its analysis. Unless we share the concept, and mean the same thing by the word 'yellow,' we cannot have any disagreement with respect to yellow–whether it could be analysed, and if so, what the correct analysis would be.

From this discussion, there is an ambiguity when talking about 'the definition' of a term, or 'agreeing on the definition' of a term. It can refer to either:

(1) the analysis of a concept, or

(2) how the term is used–on what concept the word refers to.

If we say that (dis)agreement on criteria presupposes agreement on definition, this can only refer to 'definition' in the second sense, i.e., agreement on the meaning or use of a term–on what concept the term is used to refer to. In the first sense of 'definition'–that is, the correct analysis of a concept–we can (dis)agree on criteria for a concept without agreeing on its definition or whether or not it has a definition.

There is, therefore, a difference between defining a term and giving its criteria. One can distinguish four different ideas:

(1) *Criteria*: What makes something so in the way that a woman's shape makes her sexy, the same way a car's reliability makes it popular or honesty makes one a good person.

(2) *Defining characteristics:* the way in which a person's ability to lift 100 kg of weight defines his strength.

(3) *Causal characteristics:* What causes something to be what it is, as the reason someone is referred to as strong because of lifting weights everyday or that one has the right genes.

(4) *Indicating characteristics:* Something that is an indication that something else is the case, but neither causes it to be what it is nor defines it, nor makes it what it is as considering

a car good by looking at the seams. If these seams are narrow and evenly uniform in width, the car would be considered good and if not, it is not good.

It is therefore important that we distinguish the meaning of a term from its criteria. A criterion used for gauging a good car is different from the meaning of a 'good car.' It is easy to think that if we disagree about what makes a car good–for example, you think it is its fuel economy and reliability, while I think it is speed and comfort–that we are disagreeing about the meaning of good car. Unless we agree on the meaning of a 'good car,' we cannot possibly disagree over what makes a good car, i.e. criteria. For unless we have the same concept 'good car'–that is, we mean the same thing by the words 'good car'–we will not be talking about the same thing when we 'disagree' over whether or not this is a good car.

When we disagree on whether F is a good film or not, what is the disagreement about? It may be a disagreement about what makes a good film, i.e. the good characteristics of a film. In order to disagree about that, we must both mean the same thing by a 'good film.' Imagine that by a 'good film' you meant a commercially successful film whereas I meant one that is aesthetically pleasing. In such circumstances, when you say it is good you probably mean it will be *commercially successful*, whereas in saying it is not good, I mean it is not *aesthetically pleasing*.

If we mean different things by 'good film,' then we are not talking about the same thing when we talk about a 'good film,' and there may in fact be no disagreement between us at all. Indeed, I may agree that the film will be commercially successful, and you may agree that it is aesthetically not pleasing. Hence, there would be no disagreement about whether it was a good film or not because we mean different things by 'good film.'

For there to be a disagreement about the criteria for something good, interesting, etc., we must be talking about the same concept, i.e. we must mean the same thing when we say that something is 'good' or 'interesting.'

To share the concept 'good' and thereby agree on its meaning is not to say that we must agree on the definition of 'good' or that we must think that a definition is possible.

Two Types of Disagreement

Given that disagreement is possible only if there is an agreement on the meaning of a term–only if there is a shared concept–it is clear that there are two fundamentally different types of disagreement that are possible. Let us illustrate this with an example:

Let us suppose that two people disagreed on whether X was a good car or not. We have already seen that when you say that X *is a* good car, there are two very different kinds of propositions, facts or judgements on which the criteria that "X is a good car" is based:

(1) That X has the properties E, R and S [economical, reliable, and safe].

(2) That E, R and S 'produce' the goodness, i.e., are *prima facie* good.

The first of these–that X has the properties of E, R and S–is clearly a particular contingent and *a posteriori* judgement: it is about this particular car. Though this car may have these properties, it might as well not have them and might not come to have them in the future. Also, we would know that this car has these properties only on the basis of someone's observations. Whereas the judgement (2)–that these properties make a car good–is universal, necessary and *a priori*: it is not just about this car, but any and all cars; it cannot be true today and false tomorrow, and it is not based on anyone's observation.

If you say that X is a good car and I say that it is not, it should be clear what the two different sorts of disagreement are: (1) We can be disagreeing on the first sort of fact, that this car is in fact economical, reliable and safe, even though we are in complete agreement about what makes a car good. That is, we may agree that a car is good if and only if it is E, R and S. Nevertheless, if we disagree on whether this car has in fact all those things, then we will also disagree on whether this is a good car. If I think that it is E, R and S and you think it is not, then I will think that it is good car while you will think that it is not. Though this agreement is in one sense factual, and can only be solved by resolving the factual questions about what the actual characteristics of this car are, we will also disagree about the resultant goodness of this car.

(2) We could agree on whether this car is E, R and S i.e. we could both agree that it is all three, and yet still disagree on whether it is a good car. For example, you consider E, R and S as the only things that matter in determining whether a car is good while I think that the looks of the car are also important. Since we agree that the car is not very attractive, and I am of the opinion that its beauty matters and you do not, I may conclude that the car is not good, while you think otherwise.

In this case, the disagreement is not a factual one but rather a disagreement about the value judgements. While the first sort of disagreement, over factual matters or empirical facts (whether the car is reliable or not) can be settled by means of empirical observations, the second kind of disagreement–whether looks are important or not–cannot be.

Similarly, when we disagree on whether some action by Sandra–for example about breaking a promise–was right or wrong, there are the same possibilities. When we say something she did was resultantly wrong, this will involve two different kinds of judgement:

(1) that this act had certain first order characteristics; and

(2) that these first order characteristics are right-making or wrong-making characteristics.

The first is a particular, contingent and non-moral judgement; it is knowable *a posteriori*; while the second is a universal, necessary, and moral judgement, which can only be made *a priori*.

Hence, if we disagree on whether what she did was wrong, the issue here would be on whether or not she did break her promise. You may say she did, while I would think she did not. We may agree that it is wrong to break a promise under certain circumstances, but not wrong under other different circumstances.

Let us take a specific example.

Suppose Randie borrowed Kshs. 1,000 from Brian and promised to return it on the first day of the month but then finds out before that date that Brian obtained this Kshs. 1,000 by cheating Esther-Joy and so he decides not to return the money to Brian as he had promised, saying the money should be given to Esther-Joy who had been cheated out of the money by Brian.

You may think that what he did was wrong, while I think it was not. The reason for this disagreement could be that you do not think that Brian got this money by cheating Esther-Joy; rather it was someone else who did it although I think it was Brian. Therefore, Randie was justified in not giving him back the money. The disagreement here is not a moral disagreement? We would be disagreeing over a matter of fact: whether or not Brian got this money by cheating Esther-Joy. We may be in perfect agreement that if Brian had obtained this Kshs. 1,000 by cheating someone out of it, Randie should not have given it back to him even though he had promised to do so. Since our disagreement is over the non-moral facts, whether this money was obtained by cheating someone, we would be disagreeing over the resultant moral judgement. That is, whether or not, Randie actually ought to have given the money back to Brian as he had promised; whether or not Randie was obliged to keep his promise.

The second kind of disagreement would arise if we mutually agree on the fact that, Brian got the money by cheating Esther-Joy. Also, if I conclude that Randie was not wrong in not keeping his promise to Brian, while you say he was. That even if by cheating Esther-Joy, Randie got the money, Randie still ought to have kept his promise and returned the money. If he borrowed the money from Brian on the understanding that he would return it on the first day of the month, then that is what he ought to have done. It was therefore resultantly wrong for him not to have done so.

The nature of this disagreement is a different kind *vis-à-vis* the first disagreement. Here, the disagreement is one of moral judgement, a disagreement over moral principles, which has nothing specifically to do with Brian and Randie. It has to do with a certain universal moral judgement. Something obtained by cheating someone else nullifies the *prima facie* obligation to keep one's promise while you think otherwise. While the first disagreement on whether Brian got the money by cheating someone can be settled by doing some empirical research, the second disagreement cannot be settled in that way because it is a moral disagreement.

Hybrid Judgements

Let us consider further judgements like "What Brian did was wrong" or "Brian is a good person." Are these moral or value judgements? It has been noted above that though they look simple, they are in fact complex. They rest on or contain two completely different kinds of judgements: (a) particular, factual and non-moral judgements, that certain things have certain first order properties; and (b) universal, moral judgements, that these first order properties make things good, bad, right or wrong.

Hence, these two judgements together involve three levels of issues:

(1) particular, concrete entities i.e. Brian or some action of his,

(2) first order properties i.e. his honesty, generosity, or his action being a lie, and

(3) second or higher order properties, i.e., goodness, rightness or wrongness.

The first proposition–that Brian is honest–relates to (1) and (2); the second proposition–that honesty makes one good–relates to (2) and (3).

But what about the judgement "Brian is a good person" or "what Brian did was wrong?" These arouse curiosity because they seem to relate to (1) and (3). But (1) and (3) are not related directly; they can only be related via (2). Hence, statements of this kind are what we can call 'hybrid' judgements: they go from particulars to second order properties, leaving out the connecting element; the first order properties.

It may seem obvious that statements like "Brian is a good person," or that "What he did was wrong" are certainly moral judgements. A little reflection will show that they are not, although they involve, in the sense of resting on, moral judgements. A moral judgement is universal and necessary, but such hybrid judgements are neither of the two. The fact that Brian is a good person is a particular fact; it is about Brian only and nothing else. Also, the fact that an action of Brian was wrong is a particular fact; it is about a particular act of Brian and nothing else. Hybrid judgements are therefore not moral judgements.

Further, they are clearly contingent, as can be seen in the case of the 'weakest link" principle. The hybrid judgement that *Brian is a good person* involves the following two judgements: the particular, contingent and non-moral judgement that Brian is honest; and the universal, necessary and moral judgement that honesty makes one a good person. This could be represented as follows:

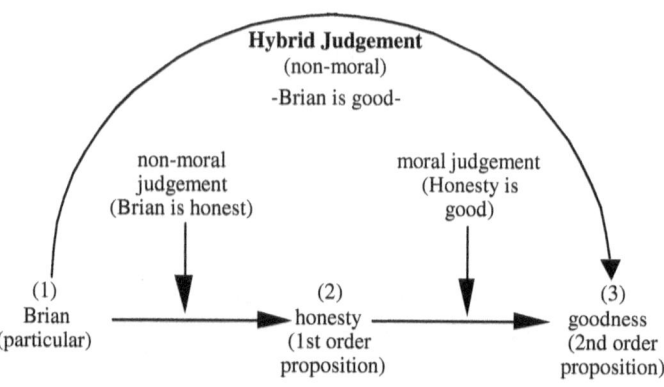

The connection between (2) and (3) is *necessary*, but the connection between (1) and (2) is *contingent;* and just as the strength of a chain is limited by its weakest link, so this chain of judgements is only as strong as its weakest link. Since contingency is 'weaker' than necessity, the whole (hybrid) proposition judgement, which connects (1) and (3), is contingent. This is correct: that Brian is a good person is clearly not a necessary fact, for he could easily become a bad person. For anyone who is honest is necessarily a good person, and that Brian or any other individual is honest and therefore *good* is contingent. Since moral judgements are necessary, we can say that any judgement that is contingent, is therefore not a moral judgement; hence, we can say the judgement like "Brian is a good person," is not a moral judgement.

However, it is important to note that as practical moral agents, and as individuals who have to make decisions about what we actually ought to do in certain situations, what we are ordinarily concerned about are questions of resultant rightness or wrongness. So, when we ask whether Brian is a good person or whether what he did was right or wrong, we are fundamentally interested in the resultant aspect. We are not just interested in knowing whether breaking a promise is *prima facie* wrong, but in knowing whether what Brian did was, everything considered, resultantly wrong.

Part 2
Two Theories of Ethics

8

The Basic Teleological Principle

There are three different types of ethical theories (1) Act-Utilitarianism (2) Deontology, and (3) Rule-Utilitarianism.

What is meant by an ethical theory? It is an attempt to give a general answer as to why a certain action is wrong or right. A theory of ethics is a hypothesis about an answer to the question why an action is right or wrong or why it ought or ought not to be done. An ethical theory also tries to give a general criterion for rightness or wrongness, that is, some general right or wrong characteristic(s) that would always be what makes an action right or wrong.

Act-Utilitarianism may be considered, one of a number of theories that can collectively be called *teleological*. The idea behind teleological theories of ethics is that, the only thing that is relevant in determining whether an action is right or wrong are the consequences of that action. Thus, such views are sometimes called *consequential theories*.

Utilitarianism is one type of teleological theories, the other being *ethical egoism*. Egoism can be considered as a teleological view because it states that an action is right if, and only if, it has the best consequences for *me*, whereas utilitarianism says that an action is right if, and only if, it has the best consequences for *everyone* or the *majority*. But since utilitarianism is the most important type of teleological theory, we can use 'teleological' and 'utilitarianism' more or less interchangeably.

Utilitarianism, sometimes referred to as *ethical universalism*, had its heyday from the late 18th century through to the last quarter of the

19th century. Its three classical proponents were Jeremy Bentham, John Stuart Mill and Henry Sidgwick. The chief architects of ethical egoism were Epicurus, Thomas Hobbes and Friedrich Nietzsche.

The basic idea underlying teleological or utilitarian theories of ethics is the *Basic Teleological Principle (BTP)*. It asserts that:

> An action is right, and hence the one which we ought to do if, and only if, it will have the best consequences.

In other words:

> The right action is the best action.

By 'best action' here we mean the best amongst all the alternatives open to the agent. Thus, it is possible for an action to have the best consequences of all the alternatives, and be the right act, even though it has bad consequences.

How can an act have, on balance, bad consequences and also have the best consequences and therefore be the right thing to do according to utilitarians? 'Best' is a strictly relative term. It means 'better than any other'. If all the alternatives have bad consequences, the one that has the least amount of bad consequences will certainly be the best; even though it may itself have, on balance, bad consequences.

Is the Basic Teleological Principle a (BTP) Truism?

The basic teleological principle can seem so self-evidently true as to be almost a truism. This is because BTP asserts that whenever you have to decide what is the right thing to do, you should always do that which is the best. The utilitarian might ask, "Can anyone suggest that when faced with a choice between doing A and B even though A is the better thing to do, that it might be right to do B?" To the utilitarian that seems absurd. If A is the best, then certainly that is what ought to be done.

One thing may appear to be the best thing to do, for example, committing euthanasia, though a look at the long-term consequences would indicate otherwise. What the utilitarian asserts is that if everything is taken into account and it is agreed that a certain course of action would be the best, then how can one possibly question whether it is the right thing to do? The utilitarian would say that one should always do something which has, everything considered, the best consequences.

It is on the basis of the BTP that the fundamental issues of ethical theory rest. It is the principle, which the deontologist challenges. It is about its compatibility or incompatibility with this principle that some of the most fundamental questions concerning the third basic ethical theory–Rule-Utilitarianism–arise. In other words, a crucial question to ask of any rival theory of ethics is whether or not it is compatible with the BTP. Put differently, are there times when we morally ought not to do that which would have the best consequences; rather what we know will not be the best thing to do?

Consider a concrete example. Imagine you are a farmer and you find out that insects are ruining a large portion of your crops and so you consider using a certain insecticide to control the pests. That would certainly be the right thing to do. Assume you also found out that although using this insecticide would increase your yield, it would leave traces of poison in the crops, which would be harmful to consumers. What should you do?

Let us consider this from a broader perspective; from the point of view of a government official who has to decide government policy as to whether or not to allow the sale and use of this pesticide, so that we can ignore the question of the individual farmer's gain.

If the government allows the use of the pesticide, it will mean not only greater profits for the farmers but also more food in the country. Although its use will definitely mean more food for more people–at least in the short run–it might well be that in the long run its bad consequences might outweigh the good. There could be two reasons for this. One, the chemical used may poison people. Two, the insects destroyed by these chemicals will develop resistance so that eventually these insecticides will have no effect on them. At this point, we will be worse off than we were before we even started using the pesticides. So, should the government official allow the use of this pesticide or not?

The point here is that whatever the official decides to do, it will clearly be based on utilitarian considerations. To decide the right course of action is to decide the best course of action–which will have, in the long run, the best consequences. We might say that although using them would have the best short-term consequences, we should nevertheless not allow its use because in the long run, it will have more harmful consequences. That is, poisoning of people and long term shortages of food due to the inevitable resistance to the pesticide if we use it versus the less immediate increase in food production if we do not use it. But this will still mean that our decision is based on a consideration of the consequences.

The "Subjectivity" Problem

When utilitarians say that an act is right if, and only if, it has the best consequences, do they mean the action that *has* the best consequences or the action that *is likely* to have the best consequences, or the action that the agent *believes* will have the best consequences?

There are three different cases to consider here. The first one is: Suppose someone drives his car from subsidiary road onto a main road without checking to see whether there are any oncoming vehicles. We are apt to say that his action is unwise. But he may reply:

> I thought you were a utilitarian and that as a utilitarian, you held that an action is right if, and only if, it has the best consequences. Now there was no car on the main road when I crossed it–though I didn't have prior knowledge–and my action had no bad consequences and had some good ones like saving a little time. Hence, from amongst the alternatives open to me–stopping or not stopping–my action of not stopping but driving straight on had the best consequences, and on the basis of your theory of utilitarianism, it was the right thing to do.

Is this a good argument against utilitarianism? It is important to note the nature of this argument. It is what in philosophy called a *reductio ad absurdum,* and has the following form: If your theory was correct, the following consequence would be true (in this case, that it would be alright to drive across a main road without looking); but that clearly is not true (that is, it would not be alright to drive like that); hence, your theory cannot be correct. The more general structure of this reasoning is what is known, in logic as *modus tollens:*

If P then Q
Not Q
Therefore Not P

This is one of the most elementary forms of argument, not only in philosophy but also in common sense. If you can show that your opponent's views lead to conclusions, which he himself will not accept, then you have shown that his original view cannot be correct. You will notice that we have constantly used this form of argument in the text.

One way of dealing with the question at hand is to say that when we consider what is best, and hence right according to the utilitarian, we have to consider such issues as risks. These are possible consequences with varying degrees of risks and possible consequences with varying degrees of probability. In crossing the main road from the side road, we know that there is a likelihood or probability of a car driving along the main road, and if that is the case, the consequences might be disastrous as there is the possibility of a road accident. This risk is something that utilitarians must take into account.

The risk is not by itself an actual consequence, but the concept of risks, i.e., probable consequence, is essentially a teleological concept because it is concerned with consequences, though with their probability rather than with their certainty. One could say that whenever we make a decision about what to do in the future–as opposed to evaluating something that we had done in the past–we are always, to some degree, going to be concerned about probability. This is because we can never know for certain what the consequences of our actions will be.

The second case is as follows: Imagine a doctor who treats a patient with penicillin without being aware that that particular patient is allergic to penicillin. Suppose further that the patient dies as a result of being given the penicillin. Is what the doctor did wrong? If we consider the consequences, his action certainly had worse consequences than the alternatives, which would have been to use an alternative drug or none at all, either of which would probably have had better consequences than what he did. Hence, what he did had worse consequences than any of the alternatives that were open to him. But common sense tells us that what he did was not wrong, even though it was not the action that would have had the best consequences.

The above constitute a serious objection to utilitarianism and we might be forced to modify, refine or reformulate utilitarianism to read:

> An action is right if, and only if, the agent has a reason to believe it will have the best consequences, that is, if it is the action that, on the basis of the information available to him, he believes would have the best consequences.

Consider the reverse case. Imagine a doctor in the same circumstances with an ill patient and with a stock of penicillin, which he has no reason to believe will not cure the patient who, though unknown to the doctor, is allergic to the drug. Instead of giving the patient the drug, the doctor takes it and sells it on the black market and leaves the patient with no treatment, and that the patient by a stroke of luck recovers from the illness without any medicine. In this case, what the doctor did was in fact the best thing because had he given the patient the penicillin, the patient would have died, whereas without the medicine the patient lived. Would it be in order to say that what the doctor did was right? We certainly would not praise him for such an action. However, we might say that accidentally or inadvertently, his action had the best consequences, but we would not say that he was acting rightly in doing what he did. In fact, we would want to say that his action was wrong.

The answer might be to distinguish between an 'objective' and 'subjective' sense of 'doing what is right or wrong'. In the objective sense, 'doing what is right' means 'doing what in fact has the best consequences,' whereas in the subjective sense, 'doing what is right' means 'doing what you believe will have the best consequences'.

This is, in any case, not a serious problem for the utilitarian. He could quite consistently say, accepting our distinction between the objective and subjective sense of right, that what we aim for is still the objectively right act, and that to him, is the action that will have the best consequences. The utilitarian would say the guiding principle on the basis of which we will try to decide what we ought to do is still the BTP; that we will take the action which will have the best consequences. Ultimately, we can only do what we believe will have the best consequence and we can only act on the basis of information that is available to us. We cannot act on the basis of facts of which we are genuinely and totally unaware of. If the beliefs on which we decide what will have the best consequences are correct, then our act will have the best consequences. That does not alter the fact that the principle upon which we make our decision is the utilitarian principle or the BTP, if utilitarianism is correct.

The problem of 'subjectivity' will equally arise for all ethical theories. It is always the case that we can only do what we believe or think is the right thing to do. After finding out as much as we can on any theory, it is possible that the beliefs on which our moral decisions rest may be false, in which case our action would–'objectively'–not be the right thing to do. Yet, we would not, in such cases, necessarily want to say that the person had acted wrongly.

Finally, the third case: Imagine that I promise to meet you on your arrival at the airport but I am given the wrong time by the airline, and get there at 10 p.m. instead of 6 p.m. In such a case, I would fail to keep my promise to meet you at the airport. But assuming that I had no way of knowing that I had been misinformed, there is no way I could have been there on time.

The issue would be: Did I fail to do the right thing, that is, keep my promise by failing to meet you on arrival? *Objectively*,yes; *subjectively*, no. Again, all I can possibly do is what I believe will be fulfilling my promise. The fact that I fail to do this, through no fault of my own, does not mean that I acted wrongly. It remains true that what I ought to aim at here is to keep my promise 'objectively'! But all that I can do is keep it 'subjectively' that is, keeping my promise.

Thus, the deontologist who has a different view of promising from the utilitarian could say, consistent with the problem of subjectivity, that it is an ultimate ethical principle that one has a *prima facie* obligation to keep promises. Based on this, the utilitarian would not agree. However, even in the case of a deontologist, it is also true that all I can ever do is what I believe will be the keeping of a promise.

Hence, the problem of subjectivity is in no way peculiar to utilitarian theories of ethics. If it is an argument against utilitarianism, it will be an equally good argument against any other theory; and if it is not an argument against these other theories, it is not an argument against utilitarianism.

9

Deontological Theories of Ethics

The deontologist challenges the utilitarian by arguing that the utilitarian theory cannot account for many common moral judgements concerning such things as the obligation to keep promises, to tell the truth, to be honest, or to punish only the guilty. For example, if we ask the utilitarian why, one ought to keep promises, the utilitarian would say, it is because keeping promises generally has better consequences than breaking them. Suppose I have promised to lend Brian Kshs. 1,000, but before I fulfil my promise, I meet Randie who asks for the same amount, and if I give it to him I will not be able to give it to Brian. What should I do and how do I make the right decision?

Barring special circumstances, such as Randie is in desperate need of the money and may be seriously hurt if he does not get it right then, while Brian's need for it is much less urgent, we would in such a case probably agree that if I had promised to give the money to Brian, then that is what I should do.

But the question is: why, according to utilitarianism, should I give the money to Brian as I had promised rather than to Randie? It can only be because giving it to Brian will, everything considered, have better consequences than giving it to Randie. For if I give it to Randie after promising Brian, Brian is likely to be very angry and may not trust me in the future and may tell other people, something which may have a bad effect on my reputation. This sort of reason–the bad consequences of not keeping a promise–is the only reason, which the utilitarian can cite why I should do what I had promised to do.

We note that for the utilitarian, the fact that I have promised to give Brian the money is not, itself, morally relevant. It is relevant only to the extent that it will have an effect on the consequences, for example, causing Brian to no longer trust me, ruining my reputation, etc. This is because utilitarianism, as an ethical theory is entirely future-looking. That is, only what will happen, in the future, can be relevant in deciding what to do now. The fact that I have promised–which is in the past–is not relevant at all. It is only extrinsically relevant if the fact that I had promised to do a certain thing *will* have some effect on what I do.

The utilitarian might argue that one bad consequence of my not keeping my promise is that my conscience would bother me, and that I should to take that into consideration when deciding whether I should to keep the promise or not.

However, if the utilitarian theory was in fact correct, then, if in the sort of case we have imagined, the utilitarian decides that the consequences of breaking the promise would be better than keeping it, then there is no reason why his conscience should bother him in the first place. This would be so because, according to his theory, he would not be doing anything wrong in breaking his promise. In this case, if his conscience does bother him then that clearly implies that he thinks what he did is indeed wrong. But if he really accepts his own theory–that he should only do that which has the best consequences–then his action would not be wrong, and his conscience should not bother him. In short, the fact that his conscience does bother him clearly shows that he does not really accept his own theory.

The deontologist argues that the utilitarian view cannot account for our ordinary judgements. Renowned deontologists include W. D. Ross, Thomas Reid and Richard Price.

On the above example, the deontologist would argue that apart from any consideration of consequences, the fact that you have promised is morally relevant; it constitutes a moral reason for doing what you have promised to do. In other words, it constitutes a *prima facie* obligation to give Brian the money. Equally, we could say that having promised to give Brian the money constitutes a right-making characteristic, and breaking the promise, a wrong-making characteristic.

It should be noted that the deontologist is not saying that if you make a promise on X, you ought to keep it no matter what. That is a position that may be held by a formalist such as the German philosopher Immanuel Kant but it is not held by a deontologist such as W. D. Ross.

What the deontologist says is that having promised to do action X creates a *prima facie* obligation to do the action X, which exists independent of the consequences. But the deontologist does not deny that other considerations may be relevant in determining what I actually ought to do. These other considerations certainly may include consequences.

Thus, if I have promised to loan you some money on a certain day, and while on my way to fulfil the promise, I come across someone in urgent need of my assistance such that helping him precludes my keeping my promise to you, I would be justified in breaking my promise. The *prima facie* obligation to keep a promise can be outweighed by a stronger and conflicting obligation to do something else, for example, if the consequences of keeping my promise were extremely bad. The fact that I have promised to do X, by itself, counts and I would be justified in breaking the promise only if the consequences of breaking it are considerably better than the consequence of keeping it. The consequence of breaking the promise must outweigh the intrinsic wrongness of promise breaking. It is the intrinsic wrongness of promise breaking which the utilitarian denies. He says instead that having promised to do X counts only to the extent that it has some bearing on the consequences. The deontologist, therefore, does not deny that consequences are morally relevant, he only denies–what the utilitarian asserts–that the consequences are the only things that matter.

We can now explain why the BTP seems self-evidently true, even when, it may not be true at all. In situations where consideration of the consequences is the only thing that is relevant–as was true in our example on whether or not to use the pesticides–then the right thing to do would be whatever has the best consequences. For, as the deontologist says, consequences are morally relevant. If the action in question is not intrinsically good or bad, then the only thing that would matter would be the consequences.

The point here is that many actions are of this sort whereby the act itself is in and of itself neither right nor wrong so that the only consideration that is relevant is a consideration of the consequences. And in so far as we are thinking about such cases, then the BTP will be self-evident and unquestionably true.

The deontologist would say that, though the consequences are relevant, they are not the only considerations. Facts about the past–such as having made a promise to do x–are also relevant and when such considerations are present, the consequences would not be the only things that are relevant.

Hence, BTP, which says that consequences are the only things that matter is to the deontologist false. But since we are often liable to consider the question as to whether this principle is true or not by considering cases where consequences are the only things that are relevant, it can appear to be true. However, once we examine things, which may be intrinsically right or wrong, we can see that BTP is by no means true and may, in fact, be false.

Deontology and Teleology: The Logical Difference

There is thus a fundamentally logical difference between the deontologist and the teleologist. The deontologist would say that there are several ultimate intrinsic obligations, such as keeping promises, telling the truth, being honest, helping others in need, etc. The teleologist, on the other hand, would say that there is only one ultimate intrinsic obligation; to do that which will have the best consequences. All other obligations are derived from this one obligation. The deontologist recognises the *prima facie* obligation to do that, which has the best consequences as one among many ultimate obligations. But he would also say that there are other ultimate obligations, such as the obligation to keep promises and to tell the truth, which are completely independent of the *prima facie* obligation to do that which has the best consequences.

Epistemological Difference

There is also an epistemological difference between the two theories concerning obligations such as keeping promises. The utilitarian would say that such obligations are based upon one principle–that of doing what has the best consequences. Therefore, if you ask "why is it wrong to break this promise?" the utilitarian must answer, "Because that will have worse consequences than keeping it". Whereas if you asked a deontologist he would say: "It is wrong because it is wrong; there is no other reason why it is wrong. Breaking a promise, is in and of itself, a *prima facie* wrong and that is all there is to it."

If you ask the deontologist how one knows that this is so, the deontologist will say that if one understands the matter and thinks about it, he will 'see' by 'intuition' akin to such intuitions as "two parallel lines will never meet" or that when two straight lines cross the opposite angles are equal, that it is *prima facie* wrong to break a promise. In the case of promise breaking, the teleologist would resort that it is wrong because doing so will have worse consequences than keeping it. The deontologist would, however, argue that this answer cannot account for many of our moral judgements, which we accept as true.

Another example: Imagine that you run a small business and a customer accidentally gives you more money than required. Should you return it to the customer, and if so, why? Common sense tells us that you should return it because doing so will, everything considered, have better consequences than keeping it. If the customer discovers his error and demands to be refunded, it will be embarrassing as well as harmful to your business. Whereas if you return it, even before the customer discovers that he has made the mistake, the customer will be impressed with your honesty and may tell others, who are more likely to continue patronising your store.

But the deontologist would inquire whether the customer is aware that he has given you more money and that it might be better to return it for the sake of your reputation. The situation may be that you stand to benefit by not returning it. It might be that the benefit that you and your family may get from keeping the money, especially if it is a large amount, is likely to be greater than any benefit that would result from returning it. It is easy to imagine circumstances in which keeping the money would have better consequences, everything considered, than returning it. Nevertheless, we would still be inclined to think that you ought to return the money. The deontologist would say that this is something, which the utilitarian cannot account for. The fact that there are cases where it would have better consequences to return the money is quite irrelevant.

Right or Wrong Independent of the consequences versus Right or Wrong, No Matter What the Consequences

From the above discussion, it is clear that when the deontologist says that breaking a promise is, in and of itself wrong, this means wrong independent of the consequences and not that it is wrong no matter what the consequences. When the deontologist says that breaking a promise is wrong he means that the wrongness is intrinsic to the act of promise-breaking and is in no way determined by consideration of the consequences. In other words, as far as the intrinsic *prima facie* wrongness of promise-breaking is concerned, the consequences are irrelevant. The deontologist could say, then, that promise-breaking is a *prima facie* wrong no matter what the consequences; the fact that some act involves breaking a promise is always and necessarily a reason for not taking that action. Hence, the deontologist could say that any and all acts of breaking promises are necessarily *prima facie* wrong.

We note that the deontologist is not saying that breaking is a promise is wrong no matter the consequences. That is, it is always resultantly–on balance, everything considered–wrong to break a promise. Although it is always *prima facie* wrong to break a promise, there may be cases where keeping a promise would have disastrous consequences, whose *prima facie* wrongness would outweigh the *prima facie* or intrinsic wrongness of breaking the promise.

Thus, if you are on your way to fulfil a promise and meet someone injured in a road accident who needs to be taken to the hospital, you have a strong *prima facie* obligation to help that person, even though doing so means breaking your promise. The *prima facie* obligation to keep your promise, however, still exists but is outweighed by your *prima facie* obligation to help the injured person. This is just like a situation where a 1-kilogramme weight on a scale continues to exist and to exert its force even if it is outweighed by a 2-kilogramme weight on the other side of a scale. The *prima facie* obligation to keep your promise may 'weigh' +5, while the obligation to help the injured person may 'weigh' +10, so that on balance, your obligation is +5 to help the injured person.

This example illustrates the point that, although we have an obligation to keep our promise *independent of the consequences*, we do not have an obligation to keep our promise *no matter the consequence*. It is important to note, however, that the deontologist is not saying that we are justified in breaking a promise just because the consequences of keeping it are bad. The consequences must be bad enough to outweigh the considerable *prima facie* wrongness of breaking a promise.

Note again, that even when we are justified in breaking a promise, we still continue to have a *prima facie* obligation to keep it. This is shown by the fact that if we could fulfil our greater *prima facie* obligation to help the injured person without breaking a promise, that would be better than helping the injured and breaking our promise.

We can illustrate the same point in relation to pain and suffering. Pain and suffering are reasonably speaking, in and of themselves, intrinsically bad. Does this mean that pain and suffering are always bad? That depends on whether you mean *prima facie* bad or resultantly bad. If you mean *prima facie* bad, then it may be true; if you mean resultantly bad, then it certainly is not.

Suppose we say that pain and suffering is bad but if you went to a dentist and he drills a decaying tooth thereby saving the tooth, which is painful, would we say it is bad? It depends on whether you mean *prima facie* bad or resultantly bad. *Prima facie,* the pain and suffering on the dentist's chair is bad; it is only resultantly not bad. In other words, taken as a whole, it is not bad. This is because although it is painful and the pain is in and of itself bad, it averts the even greater pain that you would suffer if it were not fixed, as well as enabling you to use that tooth in the future.

Put differently, one may say that though the drilling is painful, and that pain is in and of itself, *prima facie* bad, its consequences, in terms of the prevention of even greater pain and enabling the continued use of the tooth are *prima facie* good. And the *prima facie* goodness of these consequences outweighs the *prima facie* disadvantage of the pain of drilling, so that the event of having your tooth drilled, taken as a whole, is resultantly good.

To prove that the pain of having your tooth drilled is still *prima facie* bad, we need to conduct a thought-experiment. In the thought-experiment one would ask, "what if the tooth could be drilled without the pain?" If we could save the tooth and thereby prevent future pain, but without any pain from the drilling itself that would be a better alternative. This could be illustrated by analysing the drilling of the tooth, in short DT, with and without pain as follows:

(a) DT (with pain) = -5 (pain)
$\underline{+10}$ (avoidance of future pain, saving tooth, etc.)
result = $+5$ (on balance, good)

(b) DT (without pain) = 0

	+10	(everything else the same, that is, avoidance __ of future pain, saving tooth, etc.)
result	= +10	(on balance, good)

We can see that the result of drilling the tooth (DT) without pain is +10 [i.e. (b)], while drilling it (DT) with pain is +5 [i.e. (a)]. So while the latter is still, on balance, good, the former is better yet. This is because if you remove one bad thing from the whole, while the rest of the whole remains the same, the whole must become better. Thus, if we lessened the pain, without eliminating it completely, the whole would become much better, while if we increased the pain, the whole would become much worse.

Utilitarian Theory of Promising

The basic idea behind utilitarianism is that there is, ultimately, only one obligation, and that is the obligation to do that which will be the best thing to do. There may be other obligations such as keeping promises, telling the truth, not stealing. These must, for the utilitarian, be derivative as opposed to ultimate obligations i.e. be based upon the one ultimate obligation to do what yields the highest good. So for the utilitarian, there is no intrinsic obligation to keep a promise and nothing is intrinsically wrong with breaking a promise, not even *prima facie* wrong. It is wrong to break a promise if doing so will result in more harm than good.

The non-utilitarian, for example, the deontologist, could present his counter examples to the utilitarian. His examples could illustrate that, on the utilitarian theory of promising we would have no obligation to keep promises, yet our moral common sense clearly tells us that we do have an obligation to keep them. Thus, the non-utilitarian would argue:

> Suppose Brian requests to borrow my car next Saturday so that he can take his TV set for repair and I agree, but on Saturday, before he arrives, Randie shows up and asks if he can borrow it to meet his girlfriend at the airport, I should ask myself: what would be the right thing to do? As a strict utilitarian, there is only one consideration: which is *ipso facto* the right thing. Which would

produce the most good? Giving it to Brian, to whom I had made a promise, or to Randie who has just dropped by?

I think about it for a moment and decide that Randie's collecting his girlfriend will give him more pleasure than Brian getting his TV set fixed. And though, Brian will be disappointed in not being able to get his TV set fixed today, Randie and his girlfriend will be even more disappointed if he doesn't meet her at the airport. It doesn't matter whether my judgement here is correct; it is enough that that is how I judge things to be.

Hence, I decide to let Randie have the car. And when Brian arrives later I tell him, "Sorry [question: do I, *qua* utilitarian, have to apologise at all?], but I gave the car to Randie to collect his girlfriend from the airport because I thought that was the best thing to do."

But to the non-utilitarian, that would certainly be absurd moral reasoning. The mere fact that I think I can do more good by giving the car to Randie does not in any way justify breaking my promise to Brian. Common sense clearly confirms this: in such a case everyone recognises that we ought to keep our promise and would not be justified in breaking it for such a reason.

Here, the utilitarian objects:

I agree with you that in such a case we would not be justified in breaking our promise. But you are forgetting one very important thing – that Brian will not only be disappointed in not getting the car as Randie would also have been if you had not given to him. More than that, he will be annoyed and angry justifiably so, because you had promised to lend him the car, which you had not to Randie. Not only will Brian be annoyed, but he will also not trust you in the future. He may also remark to others that you are unreliable and can't be trusted to keep your word, which may harm your reputation.

In other words, the utilitarian will argue that you ignored a whole category of undesirable consequences, which will result from breaking your promise to Brian. These would include all those consequences that result specifically from the fact that you had promised to lend Brian the car and by giving it to Randie instead, you broke your promise. When you take these consequences into consideration, you will realise that breaking your promise did not really have better consequences than giving it to Brian. Instead, the best thing to do would have been to give it to Brian as you had promised. Not because you had promised, but since keeping it would have been the best thing to do.

Hence the utilitarian concludes, "My theory, if properly applied, does not contradict moral common sense."

This is the classical utilitarian response to the non-utilitarian's deontologist's attempted rebuttal of utilitarianism by way of counter-example. The usual deontological reply to this counter-argument takes either of the following formats: (1) He may argue that you can easily imagine cases where taking the above consequences into account and breaking the promise would still have better consequences than keeping it. Yet moral common sense would tell us that it would still be wrong to break the promise, but since the consequences of breaking it would be better, the utilitarian theory would allow us to break it.

For example, imagine that if I give Randie the car, he will do me a favour. Taking this into account, even when considering the loss of trust from Brian, it would still be better, everything considered, giving the car to Randie and breaking my promise to Brian. Yet, the deontologist will say, this will still be wrong.

(2) The deontologist will also cite cases in which these consequences cannot occur, as in the case of a deathbed promise. Suppose that a son promises his dying father that he would dispose off some of his father's property in a certain way after the father's death–say, to give his cattle to Brian, who, however knows nothing about it. But after his father's death, the son thinks that Randie would benefit more from the cattle than Brian. According to the utilitarian, the son would have no obligation whatsoever to give the cattle to Brian in whose name the promise had been made. In this case, Brian knows nothing about the promise and cannot possibly hold it against the deceased's son because he broke the promise; nor can the father, since he is deceased.

The deontologist therefore, asserts that the utilitarian consequences that result from breaking a promise cannot possibly occur in this case. Yet, we still do have an obligation to keep a deathbed promise.

In the case of a deathbed promise, since the promisee is no longer available, that is not possible, hence there is no way out of such a promise. Again, the deontologist says, that the utilitarian cannot account for such an obligation since in his theory, the obligation to keep such promises would be very weak, if it exists at all.

These are good arguments for the deontologists. But they also have an interesting defect in that they grant more to the utilitarian than they should. The question that needs to be asked is whether, given this theory, the utilitarian is entitled to appeal to the consequences as he does–to the consequences for the promisee as a result of the promisor breaking his promise to him? For the utilitarian's argument here is that the promisor has in fact broken his promise and that is why the promisee will be angry and may not trust him in future.

Has he, according to the utilitarian theory, really broken his promise? For if he has not broken his promise, then it is not clear at all that these consequences will indeed occur, or be expected to occur. If they cannot be expected to occur, then the utilitarian cannot appeal to them as a reason for keeping the promise.

Let us try to view the whole scenario from the point of view of a utilitarian promisor: he 'promises' Brian that he would lend him his car. What exactly does he mean when he says "I promise to lend you the car on Saturday?" As far as we can see, it may mean nothing more or less than this:

> When the time comes, I will consider what would be the best thing to do. If giving you the car seems to be the best thing to do, I will give it to you; if not, I won't. But one of the things I will take into account is that I have promised to give it to you and that you'll be angry if I don't, and so I will take this into consideration in deciding what to do.

We want to ask: Is he entitled to take these latter considerations into account, i.e., that the promisee will be annoyed if the promise is not kept? What we must ask ourselves is this: does the utilitarian promisor believe that the promisee (Brian) is, like himself, a utilitarian or not? Either: (1) he thinks that Brian is a utilitarian, like himself, or (2) he thinks that he is not or is not sure.

We will consider each of these in turn. However, note that the utilitarian theory of promising, if true, is true universally, i.e., for everyone, anywhere and at all times. So since our utilitarian promisor thinks that the utilitarian theory of promising is true, he must necessarily think that it is true with respect to Brian as well as himself. However, he need not think that everyone else accepts this theory. Common sense should tell him that though utilitarianism is true, it will not be true for all persons; which is why there are two possibilities, as indicated in the previous paragraph, with respect to the promisee, Brian.

Let us look at the first possibility where the promisor thinks that Brian (the promise) is a utilitarian. If Brian were a utilitarian, would I be justified in invoking these utilitarian consequences, that is, Brian being angry, etc.? This amounts to asking: Would I be entitled to expect Brian to be angry if I broke my promise because I thought Randie would benefit from the car more than Brian? If Brian really is a utilitarian and accepts the utilitarian theory of promising, he would have no reason to be annoyed if I gave the car to Randie. Because if he accepts the utilitarian theory of promising, then he must also accept that the decision I took is what I thought was best. Given that I believe he is a utilitarian, I would therefore not expect him to get angry. Indeed, none of us should really think that I have broken my promise in the first place.

In other words, suppose I have promised Brian the car, but when he comes and asks, "so where's the car?" I say, very calmly, "Oh, sorry, Randie came by a few minutes ago and I gave it to him because I thought he needed it a bit more than you did."[1] "But you promised it to me," says Brian, his ire beginning to rise, albeit a bit irrationally, for a staunch utilitarian as I know him to be. "Yes," I explain, again very calmly, seeing no reason whatsoever for any surprise or anger on Brian's part:

> But Randie asked for it and I thought he needed it somewhat more than you did. Since I know that you are a committed utilitarian, like myself, I know that you would realise that I had no

---

[1] As a utilitarian, is there any need for me to say I'm sorry here?

reason to give it to you if I thought I could do more good by giving it to Randie. I also knew that I needn't worry about your being annoyed as a result of not keeping my promise. In fact, I knew that even if I had not been able to tell you what happened and why I was not here to lend you the car, that would not have bothered you. For you would just have assumed that, like a good utilitarian, I must have come across something else that I thought would do more good than giving you the car, and that was the reason why I was not here to give it to you.

To which Brian, as a good utilitarian, should reply, "Oh, of course."

In other words, Brian, as a utilitarian, should not even ask me, when he comes, "where's the car?" expecting–as if he were one of those confused deontologists–that I am likely to give it to him. What he should ask, when he comes there on Saturday, is: "Well, is giving me the car today the best thing to do?" For his expectation of getting the car should be no more or less than his expectation that this will be the best thing for me to do. In some circumstances, that will be fairly high; in others, rather low. But in no case should he have any expectation above or beyond this.

The question is. Why should Brian bother to have someone make such a 'promise' in the first place? And how is he better off or what is the difference between having convinced me to 'promise' to give him the car than if he had just come by on Saturday hoping I would be there and lend him the car? For knowing that I am a utilitarian, he knows that I would do whatever I think will have the best consequences such that if he comes there on Saturday without me having 'promised' him the car, he would be in exactly the same position that he is in with or without a promise. As a utilitarian, I will do whatever I think will be the best.

It is clear, from this that to the utilitarian theory a 'promise' is absolutely meaningless, because it makes no difference to anyone as to the possible outcome. The very essence and purpose of a promise is to allow us to plan our future actions. It is important occasionally to know with reasonable certainty that certain persons will do certain things at a certain time, and to be able to count on that. That is why there are things such as promises and other kinds of agreements so that I can know now that I will have the use of your car on Saturday and hence, plan accordingly.

However, do I, as a utilitarian promisor, have a reason to even be there on Saturday to consider what will be regarded as the best? No. The only thing I am obliged to do, *qua* utilitarian, is that which is best. Hence, I will only be there on Saturday to consider your 'request' if I have some reason to be there. But again, that will be the case whether or not I have, on a utilitarian basis, promised to lend you the car.

One might attempt to explain the utilitarian theory of promising by saying that a utilitarian promise really amounts to the following: When I promise to give you my car on Saturday what I am really doing is promising to consider, when the time comes, whether or not that would be the best thing to do. This at least allows us to distinguish between making a utilitarian promise and not making one, for with one, you will know that I will consider your request, while without one, you would not even harbour any hopes.

Can we describe a utilitarian promise to do X as a promise to consider whether or not X is the best thing to do, when the time comes? What does it mean, from a utilitarian point of view, to 'promise' to consider your request? It can only mean–and at the risk of an infinite regress–that when the time comes to consider your request, I will do what I think will be the best. In other words, Saturday morning–if I happen to think about it, which I am certainly not committed to doing–I will ask myself: "would it be best to consider it?" If I think that it is best to consider it then I will consider it, but if I have anything more pressing to do, I will ignore it.

Again, that is just what I would do whether I had made this utilitarian promise or not. For as a utilitarian, I am committed only to do what is best. So on the basis of the utilitarian theory, we cannot say that I have promised to consider doing whatever I have promised to do for in fact, I have promised nothing whatsoever. I have merely reiterated the fundamental utilitarian principle: to do what I think is best, and that I will do equally well or badly whether I have made a utilitarian promise or not.

We note that there is a thing called "promising to consider someone's request." For example, if you ask to borrow my favourite CDs for your party on Saturday, I may say, "well, I can't promise, but I promise to consider it next Saturday." Here, I am saying that I cannot promise at the moment to lend you my favourite CDs, either because I want to think about it or because there are too many unknowns between now and then, That of course is quite okay, for I could have said: "no, I will not lend you my CDs" meaning that I will not consider it, now or on Saturday. But if I promise to consider it, then I have promised something that is to consider it. I may after considering it, decide not to lend them to you, or I may decide to lend them to you. I cannot say that *I am not even going to consider* it because it would contradict my promise to you.

The point in this is quite different from the position of the utilitarian. He cannot be said to have promised to consider what you have asked, because from his point of view, there is no such thing as a promise. It is clear that all talk about promising, from the utilitarian point of view, is sheer nonsense. For the sake of completeness, let us consider the second possibility mentioned above, where the utilitarian promisor thinks that the promisee is not a utilitarian but one of those misguided deontologists. Also let us alter our example to one in which you are borrowing Brian's car for several days on the understanding that you will fix anything that goes wrong with it in the meantime.

Now what should you as a utilitarian promisor do if you knew that Brian does not share your utilitarian principle of promising; he has never even heard of it? I think that you should inform him of your views on promising, and should say something like:

> You should know what I mean when I promise that I will fix anything that goes wrong with your car while I am using it. You should realise that what I, as a utilitarian mean is that if anything goes wrong I will consider whether or not my fixing it would be the best thing to do. If I think it is, I will fix it; if not, I won't.

Given this 'explanation' of what he means by 'promising', it is certain that Brian is not going to accept this 'promise'. He will lend you the car only if you give him the real promise that you will fix anything that goes wrong, not the nonsense that, unless he is incredibly dim-witted, he must realise it is not a promise at all. The only alternative for the utilitarian promisor then, is to deliberately keep his view of promising to himself. He 'promises' to take responsibility for any damage to the car, knowing that what the promisee understands by this is different from his own perception of it. Knowing that if he told the promisee how he understands it, the promisee would certainly not accept such a 'promise' and hence he would not get the car, the only way the utilitarian promisor could get the car would be by engaging in deliberate deception–getting the car under false pretences.

Not only would this involve such false pretences–which makes us rightly suspicious of any moral view which must be kept to oneself– but the fact that the utilitarian promisor must conceal the utilitarian nature of his 'promise' in order to get someone to accept it would clearly show that he himself recognises that his utilitarian promise is not genuine in the first place. For it is precisely because he realises this that he cannot reveal the nature of his 'promise' to the promisee.

In so far as we are trying to prove to the utilitarian that his view of promising is not really a promise at all, we have succeeded, since we have just shown him that he himself accepts our conclusion. He himself realises that his 'promise' is not a genuine one and that is why he must keep the nature of his 'promise' a secret from a would-be promisor.

On either possibility: (1) where the utilitarian promisor thinks that the promisee is a utilitarian, or (2) he thinks he is not–we get the same result, that the utilitarian promise is not a promise at all. We can therefore state this general conclusion: On the utilitarian theory of promising, there is no such thing as promising.

We note the *modus tollens* reasoning here:
> If the utilitarian theory were true, there would be no such thing as promising.

But there is such a thing as promising.
Therefore, the utilitarian theory is false.

Human Society: With or without promises or agreements

On the issue of promising, the question to ask is whether civilised society can exist without it. Promising is merely one form of agreement–giving one's word. When I promise to meet you at five o'clock, I am giving you my word that I will be there at that time. Certainly, things would be much more difficult if there were no promises or agreements, where one is able to rely on other people by virtue of their having made some agreement. This does not mean that society cannot exist without them.

Let us pursue the topic further by looking at the relationship between language and the obligation to be truthful.

We are now familiar with the two principles of belief which say that whatever a person believes, he necessarily believes that it is true–*first principle of belief*, and that no matter what a person believes, it never follows that his belief is true–*second principle of belief*. Similarly, there are two exactly parallel and analogous principles of assertion:

PA1: Whatever a person asserts, he necessarily asserts it as a truth.

PA2: No matter what a person asserts, it never follows that it is true.

We are mainly interested in PA1. What this means is that whenever a person says something, he is, by implication, also saying that it is true. Though this is ordinarily only implied, it can be made quite explicit. Thus, if you ask me what is happening to the price of your stock, and I say:

(1) It's going down.

I could just as well–or, if you express some surprise–say,

(2) It's true, it's going down.

If the matter is of great importance, I may say,

(3) I give you my word, it's going down.

Now one thing that is interesting and worth noting is that these three statements all say exactly the same thing that your stock is going down. The difference between them is merely in the degree of explicitness or implicitness of the speaker's guarantee–his word–that what he says is true. In all the three cases, he is equally guaranteeing–promising–that what he says is true; it is just that in (2) and (3), this promise is made successively more explicit. That the speaker is giving his guarantee–giving his word–that what he says is true in all the three cases, including (1) 'The stock is going down', is shown by the following:

Suppose I tell you that the stock is going down by asserting (1), and on this basis you sell all your stock, but it turns out that I was mistaken, the stock was actually going up, and as a result you lose a lot of money. Naturally, you would be very angry and you are likely to say to me, "Why the hell did you tell me the stock was going down when in fact it was going up?" It would be quite absurd for me to answer, "but I didn't give you my word that it was going down; I merely said that it was going down!" Why would this be an absurd response? It is absurd because to assert anything, with or without an explanation from the speaker, does carry with it the speaker's guarantee–his word–that what he is saying is true. This is understood on the basis of the first principle of assertion, and is confirmed by the absurdity of the above response.

In a similar way, if you request me to meet you in my office at three o'clock to discuss your examinations, and I say, "okay I'll be there at three o'clock." But at three o'clock I do not show up and when you next meet me you ask: "Why weren't you there at three as you had promised?" It would be absurd for me to reply, "Oh, but I didn't promise to be there, I merely said that I would be there!" That would be absurd because to say:

(4) I will be there,

is understood as and implies, that I have promised to be there. In other words, "I will be there" means exactly the same thing as:

(5) I promise to be there.

The only difference is that what is implied in (4) is made explicit in (5). This corresponds to the fact "The stock is down," means exactly the same as "I give you my word, the stock is down," the only difference being that the latter makes explicit what is implicit in the former.

So we may formulate the general, and very interesting, conclusion that:

    (6)   Whenever a person asserts anything, he is implicitly giving his word that what he says is true.

Giving one's word is nothing more or less than making a promise because any specific promise like in (4), which is equivalent to (5)– could just as well have been expressed by:

    (7)   I give you my word; I'll be there.

Propositions (4), (5) and (7) all mean the same thing. They differ only in that they make increasingly explicit what is contained in all three, in that the speaker is promising to be there.

On the basis of (6), therefore, we can see that human speech involves an implicit, understood promise. Whenever you speak to someone, you are in effect giving him your word that what you are saying is true. That is why when you lie to someone, the victim has a right to get angry for you have in effect broken your promise. You gave him your word that what you said was true, yet it was not; you did not keep your word. This has the interesting consequence that the obligation to tell the truth and not lie can be explained in terms of the obligation to keep promises.

Can human speech–language–exist without this implied promise to be truthful? What would it be like if there were no implied promises of truthfulness and the obligation for one to tell the truth? Would speech be worth anything? Would it serve the purpose of conveying information? For example, you ask someone what happened at a certain meeting and he says: "The vice-chancellor agreed to raise the book allowance." However, if you knew that the person speaking was in no way giving his word–promising–that what he said was true, you would ignore what he said. It would be as if he said:

(8) The vice-chancellor agreed to increase the book allowance, but I'm not saying that it is true.

That is exactly like saying something and then taking it back, and is actually a contradiction. In short, it is the same as if he had said nothing at all. But that is exactly what it would be like if when he spoke, he was not giving you his word that what he said was true: he would rather have said nothing. And if you knew that this was the case–that when he spoke he was not giving you his word that what he said was true–you would not even bother to ask him in the first place what happened at the meeting. This would be so because you would know that you cannot rely on what he said, so why would you even bother asking him?

In short, it is perfectly clear that without the implied promise of truthfulness, language–human communication–would be impossible and in fact non-existent. Language is what distinguishes human beings from all other animals. Without language, human beings *would not exist*, and neither would civilised society. But since there are such things as language and human society, we can say, by *modus tollens*, that the utilitarian theory is most certainly false.

10

Theories of Punishment

We are aware of what it means to say that breaking a promise is wrong irrespective of the consequences, but not necessarily, no matter what the consequences. Let us consider punishment and its moral justification. As with the question of promising, we will consider certain moral facts and judgements, which we accept as true. That is, if a person commits certain crimes he ought to be punished.

What is the moral justification for punishing a criminal? Some scholars argue that criminals should be treated, rather than punished. See, for example, Henry Odera Oruka's view in his *Punishment and Terrorism in Africa*. Such a view is, at face value fundamentally misguided since it involves treating human beings as if they are children or animals who have no free will or responsibility. However, given that some persons sometimes deserve to be punished, what is the basis of saying this? Why should they be punished?

As with any other similar question, we are concerned with certain data or facts and asking for an explanation for these data. There are some principles which, if true, would account for the original data. Our data, again, are certain moral judgements that we accept as true, specifically, that if a person commits a criminal act he deserves to be punished. This could be by strokes of a cane, imprisonment or execution, etc.

Basically, there are two types of justifications for punishment, i.e., the utilitarian or teleological and the deontological.

The Utilitarian Theory

The utilitarian theory of punishment (UTP) is based upon the basic teleological principle (BTP). BTP holds that the only reason why we ought to do some act is that doing so will have better consequences than not doing so. Thus, for the utilitarian, the only reason we can have for punishing someone who has committed a crime must come under one of the following headings: (1) deterrence, (2) protection of society, and (3) rehabilitation.

Deterrence: This simply means preventing further criminal acts by means of: (a) actually punishing the guilty people, and (b) creating the threat of being punished. Having laws that publicly state that if a person is found guilty of committing a specific crime then the person will be punished in a certain way could act as a deterrent. Presumably, the knowledge that one will be punished prevents deters potential criminals from doing things they might otherwise have done if there were no such laws. Actual punishment deters simply by demonstrating that people are punished for their criminal deeds. (c) Additionally, punishing the criminal is meant to deter the person from committing criminal acts again by 'teaching the person a lesson'. However, the extent to which the threat of punishment actually deters potential criminals is a matter of considerable debate.

Protection of Society: This is accomplished by removing the dangerous criminal from society, either by incarceration or by execution. If a person is behind bars or is dead then that person cannot commit any crime, at least not against the public. Notice that punishments such as caning do not have this effect.

Rehabilitation: This may, in effect, be subsumed under protecting society, since if a criminal is rehabilitated then that person is no longer a danger to society. We do not think the reason for rehabilitation is primarily for the sake of helping the criminal.

What all these utilitarian reasons for punishing have in common is that they are all future-looking. They are reasons for punishing a person based upon good that will come out of it in the future: They decrease the likelihood of other potential criminals from committing such acts in the future. The utilitarian asserts that the only reason for punishing someone is for the good it will do. What possible reason, the utilitarian would ask, could we possibly have for punishing someone other than the reason that doing so would have beneficial results?

The Deontological Theory or Retributivism

The deontologist argues that there is another reason as to why the criminal deserves to be punished. This is for the sake of retribution. Because of one's criminal acts, society ought to inflict pain and suffering on the person, as it were, to redress the peace that the person has disturbed by his criminal act. The person ought to be punished, the retributivist says, not because of any good that will result from one being punished–though that might be an additional reason for punishing him–but because of his crime.

Retributivism hence looks at the past. The criminal deserves to be punished because of what has already taken place and not because of what will happen as a result of his being punished. If punishing the person would also have some good consequences, well and good. But the fact that one deserves to be punished, which is the sole reason for punishing the person, has nothing whatsoever to do with the consequences of punishing the person. The person ought to be punished simply because he or she has committed a wrong. That is both the necessary and sufficient reason for a punishment.

Thus, the deontologist or retributivist is saying that if a person commits a criminal act, it is intrinsically right that the person be punished, whereas the utilitarian is saying that it is instrumentally or extrinsically good that the person be punished.

Utilitarianism versus Deontology

The deontologist's argument against the utilitarian theory of punishment (UTP) comes out to show that if UTP were correct, certain things would follow as logical consequences of that theory, which our moral common sense would regard as false. Specifically, that if UTP were accepted as true it would justify punishing the innocent and letting the guilty go free.

First, the retributivist points out that the deterrent effect of punishment depends not on actual punishment, but on the potential criminal's belief that a criminal has been punished. In fact, punishing the criminal is neither necessary nor sufficient for deterrence. Suppose a criminal is caught and punished, but no one knows that the person has been punished, is this going to deter anyone else from committing such a crime? Certainly not. If no one knows that the person has been punished, the punishment cannot possibly deter anyone else. This shows that actual punishment of the criminal is not by itself sufficient to deter other potential criminals. The potential criminals at least have to know that the criminal has been punished.

But assume that the public believes that the guilty person has been punished, even if the person has not really been punished at all. Maybe a fake execution is performed and the criminal is secretly let free. Will that make any difference in terms of deterring other potential criminals? Of course not. If everyone thinks that the criminal has been executed then for them to be deterred they will be deterred by a fake execution just as much as a real one. As long as they think that the fake execution was real it would have a deterrent effect on them.

This shows that it is not necessary for a criminal to be actually punished in order to deter others. In fact, what is necessary and sufficient to produce a deterrent effect is simply that they believe that the guilty person has been punished. Strictly speaking, punishing the guilty person, in and of itself, is irrelevant.

Hence, the retributivist argues, the UTP would justify the following: Assume that you are the chief law enforcement officer in a small town where a horrendous crime has been committed. You apprehend the guilty person who is tried and sentenced to death. But you are a staunch utilitarian, and you ask yourself what good would result from executing the man. For one, it will prevent the person from ever committing such a crime again. Secondly, other potential criminals may be deterred from committing similar acts by seeing what has happened to the criminal. These are the good consequences. On the other hand, this man and his family will suffer greatly and as a utilitarian that must count as a negative aspect of the execution.

But then the law enforcement officer realises that if the public believe that the person has been executed, even if he has not been, that will achieve just as much a deterrent effect as if he were really executed. So the law enforcement officer asks himself:

> Why shouldn't I stage a fake execution, thereby achieving the full deterrent effect since people will thereby believe that he has been punished for his crimes? But in reality let the man go free and send him to some very isolated place where we can be sure he will have no opportunity to commit such crimes again? Doing this will achieve all of the good consequences of actually punishing him–i.e., deterring others from committing such a crime by causing them to believe that he's been punished and protecting society by sending him to an isolated place. At the same time I will have avoided all the bad consequences of actually punishing him, i.e., making him and his family suffer.

This means that by letting the criminal go free, the law enforcement officer would be doing much more good than by punishing him and therefore according to UTP we should let him go free.

The retributivist's argument here is that from a utilitarian point of view, this reasoning would be perfectly justified. Yet, the retributivist says, moral common sense tells us that it most certainly would not be. If this man committed a horrible crime, then he ought to be punished. The fact that we can satisfy all the utilitarian benefits of punishment even though he is in fact not punished is quite irrelevant. The retributivist or deontologist would say that it is wrong to let the man go free even if we could bring about all of these good consequences by doing so.

His theoretical conclusion would be that if a person has committed a crime, the person deserves punishment for its own sake, and not because of any consideration of the consequences. If the person has committed an illegal act, it is intrinsically right that he be punished.

And this intrinsic rightness has nothing whatsoever to do with the outcome of the act of punishing the person.

The utilitarian, the retributivist asserts, would say that we would be justified in letting this person go free, but clearly this is not so; therefore, UTP is incorrect. This, in effect, is a form of argument known in logic as *modus tollens*:

>If p then q
>Not q
>Therefore, not p.

Verbally expressed the argument would read as:

>(1) If UTP were correct, the guilty man should be let free.
>
>(2) But the guilty man should not be let free.
>
>(3) Therefore, UTP is not correct.

This sort of argument constitutes both the strength of retributivism and the weakness of UTP. Retributivism, whatever its faults, does agree with, and accounts for, the data of our moral common sense, while UTP is, at face value incompatible with it. Taken singly, these arguments seem quite decisive against UTP because if we accept our moral common sense then we must reject UTP.

At the same time, there is something interesting about retributivism as an instance of a deontological theory. If a deontologist or retributivist were asked what his basis or argument for saying that it is intrinsically right to punish a guilty person, his answer would not be satisfactory. His answer will be that if you consider the matter clearly you will just 'see' that this is so. This 'perception' of moral right and wrong is sometimes called intuition. Hence the moral theory, which holds that moral truths are known by this intuition, is known as intuitionism.

The intuitionist compares moral knowledge to mathematical or geometrical knowledge. If you ask, "How do you know that opposite angles are equal?" the only answer can be, "Well, if you think about it you will just see that they must be". Similarly, the intuitionist in ethics says that if you clearly look at it, you will just see that a man guilty of a certain crime ought to be punished, and there is really nothing more to say about it. Just as a person who cannot 'see' that opposite angles must be equal would be deficient in mathematical judgement, so a person who is unable to 'see' that a guilty person deserves to be punished would be deficient in moral judgement.

As opposed to what may seem to be a rather unsatisfactory position, the utilitarian has a much better answer as to why we should punish a guilty person, arguing that doing so will have the best consequences and therefore is the best thing to do. And taken literally it seems a much more satisfying answer than simply saying, as the intuitionist/deontologist/retributivist says: It is wrong because it is wrong, and if you think about it you will 'see' that it is wrong.

Moreover, the utilitarian can come up with a reasonable answer to any moral question. Why should we punish this person? keep this promise? tell the truth? be allowed free speech, own property? etc. In all of these cases, it is because doing so will, in the long run, have better results than not doing so.

Whereas, if you ask the deontologist why we should keep promises, the deontologist will say "because it is intrinsically wrong to break them, and that is an ultimate moral truth". Why should we punish a criminal? "Because it is intrinsically right to do so, and that is another–distinct and separate–ultimate moral truth". Why is it wrong to steal? "Because it is intrinsically wrong to do so, and that is another ultimate moral principle."

One should note, therefore, that utilitarianism, as applied to the question of punishment and as a general moral theory, has certain distinct advantages over deontological theories. It is much simpler, since it bases all other moral truths upon one supreme, simple, and plausible and even seemingly self-evident principle, i.e., the BTP– that the right act is the best act. Deontology, on the other hand, must continually postulate more ultimate moral principles, for which there is no answer as to why they are true: why is it wrong to break a promise, to lie, steal, or punish an innocent man? When you ask the deontologist why these things are wrong, he can only answer: "they are wrong because they are wrong and that's all there is to say".

Note then that intuitionism is not put forward as any kind of argument by means of which to prove moral truths. For the deontologist or intuitionist, there are neither such proofs or arguments nor any need of an argument to prove that it is wrong to punish someone who is not guilty. Indeed, the deontologist would say, even looking for an argument constitutes a serious error in moral philosophy i.e., thinking that these things need or can be given any further basis.

11

Justice and the Obligation not to punish the Innocent

Let us consider another argument that the deontologist uses against the UTP, which will lead to consideration of the notion of 'right or wrong no matter what the consequences.' Though there is an obligation to punish the guilty, in and for its own sake, and though this obligation is, like the obligation to keep promises, independent of any consideration of the consequences, there is an even stronger obligation not to punish the innocent. In other words, though it is intrinsically wrong to let a guilty person go free, it is even worse to punish an innocent person.

This is reflected in most legal systems. The principle that, for someone to be convicted the evidence must show that he is guilty "beyond any reasonable doubt" or "beyond the shadow of any doubt," is common in many African and Western judicial systems. This is meant to make it extremely difficult to convict anyone of a crime. The burden of proof is on the prosecutor; an accused is presumed innocent until proven guilty. Many legal safeguards have, as their principal goal, to make it difficult to find a person guilty. Under most legal systems, the legal machinery requires the prosecution to give all evidence that it has including even those that might tend to exonerate the accused. Failure to do so would automatically lead to a verdict of not guilty. However, there is no corresponding requirement for the defence to give condemning evidence to the prosecution. Again, in most legal systems, the jury must be unanimous to get a conviction.

The rationale of such a practice is to make it onerously difficult to convict anyone of a serious crime because convicting an innocent person is thought to be much worse than letting a guilty person go free. Requiring evidence "beyond any reasonable doubt" means that there will be cases where it is highly likely that the accused is guilty, but because the evidence is not overwhelming and conclusive, the person will be declared not guilty. This means that there will be many cases of people who are in fact guilty of crimes–and of whom we are fairly sure are guilty–who must, from the point of view of the law, be declared not guilty. Otherwise if it were granted that in cases where the evidence makes it seem likely that the person is guilty than innocent then the person is declared guilty, it would mean that some innocent people could be found guilty. But since we think it is better to let some guilty people go free than have one innocent person punished for something he did not do, we try by these legal procedures and principles, to make it very difficult to convict a person of a crime. We therefore try, as far as possible, to ensure that no innocent person is ever punished.

In short, since we know that errors of judgement are bound to occur, we try to establish procedures where should there be errors, they will be in the direction of letting guilty persons go free, rather than wrongly punishing innocent people. Thus, the principle that only the guilty should be punished, and that an innocent person must never be punished, is one of the strongest of all moral principles, overriding, for instance, the principle that all guilty persons should be punished.

The Dreyfus Affair

Let us consider the next argument, which the retributivist uses against the utilitarian. Consider the case of Alfred Dreyfus, a Jewish officer in the French Army High Command in the late 19th century. He was accused of treason, found guilty and sentenced to life imprisonment on Devil's Island. Soon after, certain people in the High Command discovered that Dreyfus was innocent and that another man, whom they identified, was in fact guilty. It further turned out that the court martial that convicted Dreyfus was improperly conducted, and was aware of the evidence exonerating Dreyfus but had squashed it.

When the proof of Dreyfus' innocence was presented to the heads of the army, they simply refused to consider it. The case was eventually made into a *cause celebre* by the famous French writer Emile Zola in his tract *J'Accuse! (I Accuse!)*. This incidentally caused him to flee the country. Despite all this the argument used by those generals who had had a hand in Dreyfus' conviction and in the refusal to reverse or even reconsider the verdict, was that even if Dreyfus was innocent he could not be set free. Their argument being that for the army to admit that they had made a mistake and knowingly sent an innocent person to prison would have a disastrous effect on the morale of the military and the country as a whole.[2] How can we, the generals asked themselves, compare the suffering of this one man, Dreyfus, and his family to these terrible consequences to the morale of the Army? Clearly, the latter are much greater and much more serious. Hence, they argued that Dreyfus must remain in prison.

After many years, they were eventually forced to admit his innocence and after sometime, Dreyfus was rehabilitated into the French Army. But they were also correct in saying that admitting Dreyfus' innocence would cause great public dissent and turmoil. With his rehabilitation riots occurred, in which many were injured and some lost their lives, the careers of many politicians and military officers were ruined, it caused the fall of more than one government and, in the opinion of many historians, nearly led to civil war. And no doubt, it weakened the morale–and the strength–of the army. The suffering, loss of life and social and political turmoil caused by the controversy over the freeing of Dreyfus were great. The upheavals were many times greater than the suffering that would have resulted

---

[2] At this juncture one may want to ask the following two related questions. First question: why would it have a disastrous effect on the army's morale? Answer: Because they would be ashamed and embarrassed by it. Second question: Why would they be ashamed and embarrassed by it? Answer: Because they themselves would know that it was the wrong and shameful thing to do. Notice already, what we will discuss further later on, how this argument contradicts itself.

to Dreyfus and his family if the whole affair had been kept secret and his stay in prison uninterrupted.

This example is used as an argument against the UTP and utilitarianism in general, because it would ordinarily be accepted that in spite of the consequences of freeing him–no matter how bad they might have been–he ought to have been freed. Why? Because he was innocent! And why was his innocence so important? To keep an innocent person in prison is unjust. And what is unjust is wrong.

It is argued by the retributivist-deontologist, that according to the UTP, Dreyfus should not have been freed. But, the retributivist would say, moral common sense–which he would assume, the utilitarian would also accept–clearly tells us that he must be freed. He therefore argues that the UTP cannot be correct since it would justify things that we would all accept as wrong.

Note, that this reasoning is an example of *modus tollens*. Thus:

(1) If UTP were correct, then Dreyfus should not have been set free.
(2) But that is false: Dreyfus should have been let free.
(3) Therefore, UTP is not correct.

The response of the utilitarian to this argument would ordinarily not be to deny that Dreyfus should have been set free. The utilitarian would agree with the deontologist, and most other people, that he should indeed have been set free. In fact, unless he agrees with this moral fact–datum–there would be no possibility of a disagreement between them about which theory best accounts for it. Rather than disputing whether Dreyfus should have been freed or not the utilitarian will instead deny that UTP, if properly understood, would result in this conclusion. In other words, instead of denying proposition (2) above, he will deny proposition (1); he will say that UTP, when correctly understood, does not lead to the false conclusion that an innocent person should be kept in prison.

Now, let us consider this question: Is someone who thinks that Dreyfus should not have been freed necessarily asserting utilitarianism? The answer is no. Of course he may be, but he may also be saying that though it was *prima facie* wrong to keep an innocent person in prison because of the bad consequences that would result from freeing him he ought, everything considered, to be kept in prison.

Stated differently, the two theorists are agreeing that punishing an innocent person is intrinsically, in and of itself, wrong; wrong independent of the consequences. Therefore, the mere fact that freeing him would have worse consequences than keeping him imprisoned, by itself, does not justify keeping him imprisoned, as a genuine utilitarian would be committed to saying. Keeping an innocent person in prison is wrong and, presumably, very wrong. Hence, unless the considerable *prima facie* wrongness of punishing an innocent person is outweighed by the benefits of avoiding extremely bad consequences, he ought to be freed–i.e., it would, on balance, be wrong to keep him in prison. Thus, he is disagreeing with the utilitarian who would say that as long as the consequences of freeing him would be worse than keeping him in prison, he should be kept in prison.

Restricted versus Unrestricted Retributivism

Restricted retributivism takes the view that the wrongness of punishing an innocent person is comparable to the wrongness of breaking a promise. That is, it is *prima facie* wrong, and this wrongness can without difficulty, be outweighed by utilitarian type considerations to the contrary.

A restricted retributivist may say that Dreyfus ought to have been freed because the *prima facie* wrongness of being innocently punished is greater than the *prima facie* wrongness of the bad consequences. But the point is, he could also say the opposite–that he should be kept in prison because the wrongness of the consequences are greater than the wrongness of his wrongful imprisonment.

On the other hand, unrestricted retributivism takes the view that Dreyfus, or anyone in that situation, should be freed; that is, he ought to be freed (almost) no matter what the consequences.

This reveals something very important about the concept of justice. Justice is in fact a resultant moral concept. To say that something is unjust is not simply to say that it is *prima facie* wrong, but that it is resultantly wrong and hence ought not to occur. Since Dreyfus was innocent sending him to prison was unjust. Therefore, what we can call unrestricted retributivist position holds that it is resultantly or 'absolutely' wrong to keep him in prison. In other words, it is wrong to keep him in prison no matter what the consequences of freeing him would have been.

In effect, one thing which the unrestricted retributivist is saying is that when considering questions of justice, any and all considerations of consequences are irrelevant, so that there really is nothing as 'resultant' or *'prima facie'* rightness or wrongness in such cases. It is simply wrong, period, and therefore must not be done.

Justice as we know is a subset of morality. All questions of justice are questions of morality, but not all questions of morality are questions of justice. Hence, anything that is unjust will be wrong and anything that is just will be right. But not everything that is wrong is *ipso facto* unjust, nor is everything that is right, just. For example, it is unjust to keep an innocent person in prison; therefore it is wrong. But though it is wrong to break a promise, it would be absurd to say that is it unjust or just. For questions of breaking or keeping a promise are not matters of justice at all, but matters of morality–that is, right and wrong. Justice is only one sphere within morality.

But, justice has some peculiar logical characteristics in comparison with other moral concepts. While it is clear that though it may always be *prima facie* wrong to break a promise, this *prima facie* wrongness is not completely independent of any consideration of the consequences. As a result, this *prima facie* wrongness can be outweighed by very bad consequences of keeping it in which case it will not be, everything considered, wrong to break it. Wrongness of breaking a promise can and should be weighed, for it is just one factor in the moral situation. It contributes wrongness to any situation of which it is a part, and if there are no other morally relevant factors, it will be the determining factor. But it must be weighed against any and all other morally relevant factors–such as saving someone's life. That is why we would say, deontologists included, that though breaking a promise is wrong independent of the consequences, we cannot say that it is wrong no matter what the consequences.

But when it comes to questions of justice, the situation seems to be fundamentally different. Here, we do not want to say that injustice is wrong independent of the consequences, but that it is wrong no matter what the consequences. Because, it seems, matters of justice cannot be weighed; they are not just one factor among many in a moral situation. To say that something is unjust is already to make a resultant or final, moral judgement, that is, that it must not be done.

In fact, to say that "if an act is unjust it is therefore wrong, everything considered," is not quite right. This is because the phrase "it is wrong, everything considered" is redundant; it is already contained in the phrase "the act is unjust." When it comes to matters of justice, if an action is unjust then nothing else can or should be considered. If an act is unjust then it simply must not be allowed to happen.

We may say, that judgements about justice, unlike those about promise-breaking, issue immediately into judgements about what we ought to do. That some action involves the breaking of a promise does not immediately tell us that we ought not to do it; it simply tells us that we have one good reason for not doing it. But that some action is unjust does seem to mean, without knowing or considering anything else, that it should not be done. We have said that injustice is wrong "(*almost*) no matter what the consequences". The reason for the qualification "almost" is that we do not want to rule out the possibility of justifying injustice. If the consequences of doing what justice require were so incredibly horrendous–for example, if it literally meant the end of the human race–we might then be justified in doing what was unjust. Perhaps, such cases would constitute intolerable and insoluble moral dilemmas.

Reflections on Punishing the Innocent

The three possible positions advanced by theorists regarding punishing the innocent are: (1) The simple utilitarian view, which says that the only thing that matters are the consequences, so if better consequences will result from punishing an innocent person than from freeing him, he should be punished. (2) The restricted retributivist position, which says that though punishing an innocent person is *prima facie* wrong, if the consequences of doing so are sufficiently great, then these can outweigh the *prima facie* wrongness of punishing him and it can therefore be, everything considered, right to punish him. (3) The unrestricted retributivist view, which says that no matter what the consequences, it is always wrong to punish an innocent person.

Although the first two views differ from each other [in that while the first is a utilitarian view and the second (at least nominally) a deontological view], they both agree that there are times when consideration of the consequences will justify punishing an innocent person. And in this they are opposed to the third view, that of unrestricted retributivism, which asserts that we are never justified in punishing an innocent person, no matter what the consequences.

Let us consider the view of the restricted retributivist, as the less extreme of these other two views, with respect to Dreyfus-type cases. His position is that although he admits that the person in prison is completely innocent and is completely undeserving of punishment, he must be kept in prison because of the consequences of letting him out. Notice that we are not talking about someone in a position where were Dreyfus to be freed and his innocence admitted, the person in question will himself be ruined, but rather someone who is saying that for the 'public good' Dreyfus must remain in prison. A person in the former situation, facing the prospect of personal ruin, might have very good reasons in terms of his own self-interest, in seeing that Dreyfus' innocence is kept secret and Dreyfus kept in prison. But such reasons are not and cannot be paraded as moral reasons in the first place. That is, no one can say "I think it is morally right that Dreyfus be kept in prison because I will suffer loss of my reputation if he is released."

Yet another person could argue that Dreyfus should be kept in prison because of the 'public good', not his own private benefit. His argument could be expressed as: "We know that he is innocent, but to admit this and free him would have disastrous social and political consequences. Therefore we cannot admit his innocence publicly and set him free; we are morally justified in not setting him free."

The first important thing to note about this argument is that it cannot be and, in the Dreyfus affair, was not expressed in public; it can only be stated in private. This is the argument, which the French generals and politicians used amongst themselves and against anyone who privately challenged them. But it was not what they said publicly. In public they simply said that Dreyfus was guilty and must be kept in prison.

Why can't the argument, of the restricted retributivist or of the utilitarian, be expressed publicly? The major reason is that there would be a kind of contradiction in doing so. If the generals were to say publicly: "We know that he is innocent, but we cannot admit this publicly since doing so would have disastrous consequences," it would amount to a contradiction. They would be saying, first that they cannot admit his innocence publicly, and in the very act of saying that they cannot admit this publicly, they would be doing precisely that–admitting it to the public. If you are going to keep something secret from the public, you cannot tell them that you are going to do so without doing exactly what you say you are not going to do.

It would be as if I was to say to you "I cannot admit to you that I'm cheating you because you would never trust me." For in telling you that I cannot admit this to you I am *ipso facto* admitting it to you. I may of course tell someone else that I cannot admit to you that I am cheating you because of the consequences; but I cannot tell you. Similarly, the generals could only express their utilitarian argument to each other but not to the public, since their concern was that by doing so it would make the public react through riots.

What, then, could they publicly proclaim? Could they say that although he was innocent, they couldn't free him, because of the consequences of doing so? That is, could they say "We know that he is innocent but to actually go ahead and free him would have disastrous consequences, and so we cannot free him?" But why, according to them, would freeing him after having already admitted his innocence have disastrous consequences? It cannot be because those who would cause the turmoil think he is guilty, for he has just been proclaimed innocent. If necessary, the government in admitting his innocence, could present proof of the actual guilty person. Why then should there be turmoil if he is freed after his innocence is publicly acknowledged? Can it be because some people will think that though he is innocent he should nevertheless still be punished? But that of course would be quite absurd. No one could possibly–even logically–claim as a moral principle that an innocent person deserves to be punished. So the people who would supposedly run amok at his being freed cannot be doing so because they think that though he is innocent he should nevertheless be kept in prison.

Could the public think that though he is innocent and hence deserves to be freed, still, if he is set free, there will be turmoil so that he ought not to be freed? In other words, could the public, each individually, be utilitarians or restricted retributivists? But that would also be absurd. For if the public knew that he was innocent such that they are not going to be upset if he is freed, who else are they talking about when they say that 'they', or 'others' will be upset and cause turmoil? For there are no others.

Could the generals say, publicly, that though he is innocent he must be kept in prison because of the devastating effect his release would have on the military? Why would his release have such an effect on the army's morale? That is, what is it, which would have this effect? It is clear that it would be their knowledge that the army has knowingly kept an innocent person in prison. But if the generals publicly say "Dreyfus is innocent, but he cannot be freed because public disclosure of his innocence would have devastating effects on the morale of the army," this could be the same kind of contradiction as before. They would be saying that they cannot disclose his innocence, yet that is precisely what they have just done by making it public.

In short, the utilitarian or restricted retributivist view that under certain circumstances an innocent person must be kept in prison because of the consequences of freeing him is a view that can only be expressed secretly. But a purported moral view that cannot, by its very nature, be expressed openly cannot be an acceptable moral view. In fact, it cannot really be expressed as a moral view. The statement "though so and so is innocent and hence does not deserve to be punished, but for some utilitarian reasons he deserves to be punished" is absurd.

The only view that can appear plausible is that "though he is innocent and therefore does not deserve to be punished nevertheless, because of the disastrous consequences of not punishing him, we would be justified in punishing him." But that will also not bear scrutiny and in part appears to contradict itself, since it first says that he ought not to be punished, but then appears to turn around and say that he ought to be punished. Many persons may have wanted to see Dreyfus remain in prison simply because he was a Jew and they hated Jews. But that too could not be stated as a moral view.

This utilitarian argument also suffers from a defect similar to the corresponding utilitarian argument regarding promising. When we claim that the admission that an innocent person has been kept in prison will cause turmoil and loss of morale in the army, it presupposes that the public or at least a large part of it are not utilitarians and would consider it outrageous that an innocent person has been imprisoned. This means that the utilitarian argument acknowledges and rests upon the fact that most people are not utilitarians nor even restricted retributivists since the utilitarian's or restricted retributivists' argument assumes that people will be outraged by the disclosure that an innocent person has been kept in prison.

There are, then, apparently three different views one can have about punishment: the utilitarian view, the restricted retributivist view, and the unrestricted retributivist's view or formalist view.

Utilitarianism, Deontology and Formalism

We could broaden these three categories by distinguishing between three different types of views that one can have on moral questions in general: the *utilitarian*, the *deontological* and the *formalist*.

The utilitarian view is that only consequences count. Deontology holds that it is not only the consequences that count but also the intrinsic rightness or wrongness of the action or state of affairs. The utilitarian denies that there is such a thing as the intrinsic rightness or wrongness of actions. Finally, the formalist is someone who holds that, at least in some cases, consequences do not count at all, and that only the intrinsic rightness or wrongness of the action counts.

We could express these three possible views as:

Intrinsic	Nature of Act	Consequence
Utilitarianism	does not count	does count
Deontology	does count	does count
Formalism	does count	does not count

So far, we have considered one example of formalism, whose view is quite reasonable, that it is wrong to punish an innocent person independent of the consequences. But a person could be a formalist about other moral questions. Immanuel Kant, a great German philosopher, apparently held that it is resultantly wrong to lie, that is, that one ought not to lie no matter what the consequences. The deontologist does not say this: he merely says it is a *prima facie* wrong to lie, independent of the consequences. But a formalist, like Kant, would hold that it is always, under all possible circumstances, resultantly wrong to lie.

This kind of view, formalism, is implausible, if not contradictory. For when the formalist says that it is always resultantly wrong to lie he is, in effect, saying that it is always wrong, everything considered. So that when we come upon any case of lying we can say immediately, that it is resultantly wrong. But when we say that something is resultantly wrong, we mean that it is wrong, everything considered. Hence, the formalist is saying that any act of lying is *wrong everything considered* though he *considers only one thing–*

that it's a lie–in other words, he does not consider everything. And that seems like a contradiction.

The formalist would defend his position may be by saying that, in such cases–punishment, truthfulness, promising–one should not and cannot consider everything. These are not the sorts of things that can be 'weighed', one thing against another. If something is a lie, that is all you need to know and therefore you must not do it.

Plausible or not, this kind of view is held e.g. it is often held with regard to violence or war, and abortion. Thus, some people hold that it is wrong to use violence under any circumstances, and this in effect constitutes the position known as pacifism and the philosophy of non-violence.

Moral Views versus Moral Theories

It is worth trying to understand the difference between a moral theory and a moral view or judgement. Thus, while the disagreement between utilitarianism and deontology concerning promising is 'theoretical', the disagreement between restricted and unrestricted retributivism concerning punishment is an actual moral disagreement over what ought or ought not to be done in an actual case. Thus, if it appeared that freeing Dreyfus would have had disastrous consequences, the restricted retributivist would say that he ought to be kept in prison, whereas the unrestricted retributivist would say, "No, he must be set free, independent of the consequences." This is not a theoretical disagreement over how to account for or explain some already agreed upon moral facts. It is instead a moral disagreement–perhaps ultimate–over what is right or wrong in a particular case.

In contrast to this, the disagreement between the utilitarian and the deontologist over, for example, the nature of the obligation to keep promises is strictly theoretical. They would both claim to accept our moral common sense judgements about what should do in a particular case, for example, that mere inconvenience is not a sufficient reason for not keeping a promise, etc. Their disagreement is about the theory or principles in moral facts. The utilitarian saying that we ought to keep a promise because it will, in the long run, have better consequences than breaking it, while the deontologist saying that we ought to keep it because it is intrinsically wrong to break it. But there is no disagreement here about what we actually ought to do. In this case, it is fully agreed that we ought to keep the promise. The only disagreement here is over *why* we should keep the promise.

The deontologist will certainly agree that the utilitarian's theory would sanction certain things–letting the guilty go free if we could fake the punishment, punishing the innocent if that would deter crime, breaking a death-bed promise–that our moral common sense would not sanction. But the utilitarian would ordinarily deny that his theory would allow such things, precisely because he does not want to be in disagreement with the deontologist over these facts, which are accepted by our moral common sense. He will therefore argue that these things are not sanctioned by utilitarianism.

In contrast to this, consider the difference between the deontologist and the formalist regarding violence and war. The deontologist may say that war, as an instance of violence, is *prima facie* bad, but that certain wars, for example, the Second World War against Nazi Germany were, on balance, justified and hence, not wrong. Whereas the formalist, taking what amounts to a pacifist position, will say that violence is always resultantly wrong, no matter what the consequences or circumstances, and that World War II, as an act of violence, was therefore wrong.

Consider the terrorist bombing attacks of the twin towers of the World Trade Centre in New York and the Pentagon in Washington D.C which took place on September 11, 2001. Both the deontologist and formalist would agree that these acts of violence were wrong. A deontologist may however assert that though the terrorist attacks (as instances of violence) were *prima facie* wrong, they were nevertheless, everything considered, justified and hence not wrong. A formalist, on the other hand, would assert that the terrorist attacks were resultantly wrong no matter the consequences or circumstances that led to the attacks. It is worth noting that virtually everyone agreed that the terrorist attacks were wrong, if not evil. The only disagreement was that some adopted the formalist position whereas others embraced the deontological standpoint.

This then would be a fundamental disagreement over a moral judgement. The deontologist asserting that a certain course of action, fighting Hitler in World War II or the terrorist attack in the US, was morally justified and was therefore the right thing to do. Of the same course of action, the pacifist or formalist would hold that it was unjustified and wrong. Such a fundamental disagreement in moral judgement could not, at least in theory arise between the two different moral theories, such as utilitarianism versus deontology. For they both claim to accept the same moral judgements, *qua* moral theorists. They may have moral differences between them as individuals, but that would have nothing to do with their theoretical disagreement. Their theoretical disagreement presupposes agreement about the moral facts on which they have different theories and explanations.

Formalism: Pacifism

Further to our discussion of formalist moral views above, we have mentioned briefly that one instance in which formalist moral views have been held is with respect to violence, i.e., pacifism. The formalist view holds that certain things are wrong no matter what the consequences. With respect to justice, we said that this was not simply plausible but probably true, in that if something is unjust then it seems obvious that it is wrong no matter what the consequences. Since it is unjust to keep an innocent person in prison, it is wrong– no matter what the consequences. In other words, the wrongness of his imprisonment cannot be weighed against anything else, and thus cannot be outweighed.

Thus, in the matter of justice, it seems that this extreme view–that certain things are right or wrong no matter what–is correct. But what is worth pointing out is that this formalist view is held with respect to other issues, such as violence, and that it is not merely some wild idea cooked up by philosophers. On the contrary, it is something held in the 'real world' and certain views, which have recently been of social and political significance, embody this philosophical idea of 'wrong no matter what' and hence can only be understood by grasping that idea.

Some people would say that they are 'against' violence and would agree that it is wrong. But they would usually add that there are times when violence is 'necessary', and hence justified. In other words, they would be asserting that violence is (always) *prima facie* wrong, but sometimes is *not* resultantly wrong.

But there are other people–specifically pacifists–who say that violence is wrong no matter what the circumstances or consequences. They say that violence is always resultantly wrong, no matter what the consequences or conditions, so that one should never resort to violence: it is never justified in any way. Two famous and important people who have advocated and practised such theories of non-violence were Mahatma Gandhi and Martin Luther King. Also, one might say that Jesus Christ was advocating such a view when he said that we should 'turn the other cheek' if someone strikes us. Even if one is walking peacefully down a street doing nothing more than asking for his legitimate rights and bystanders and police start throwing things at him and kicking him, he should not use violence in response. One should not use violence even if it is for the purpose of defending oneself or one's family.

Literally this seems a rather controversial view to defend because it is not difficult to imagine circumstances in which the only way to prevent the very kind of violence that this person abhors is by using it. One sort of answer, which an advocate of non-violence might use here, is to say that violence breeds violence, and though it may seem as if you can prevent violence by using it, in the long run you will simply spawn much more violence.

Pacifism is absolutely opposed to wars: of any kind, anywhere and at all times. It does not merely assert that war is *prima facie* bad or that some war is bad, but that all wars are resultantly bad.

Yet there are situations where people used or are using horrible and profoundly reprehensible violence–for example, Adolf Hitler or Idi Amin–where it seemed that the only way to stopping them is by resorting to violence. To say that people should have sat back and let

Hitler take over the world because violence is always wrong and never justified seems a difficult view to fathom, morally, let alone accept.

Similarly, assume that someone is about to murder your wife and children, and that the only way to stop him is by using violence–which, let us assume, you could do. Pacifism would have it that even in such a situation you should not resort to violence but should instead try to persuade him, even if this means that you and your family are all killed and the murderer walks away. This view, as we have already noted, is most implausible.

It is worth distinguishing, what we might call an intrinsic formalist view from an extrinsic formalist view. The former asserts that it is wrong to use violence. An extrinsic formalist (pacifism or non-violence) says that violence is wrong and unjustified because it will inevitably lead to more violence. You may think that by using violence to stop Hitler or prevent someone from killing your family, you are preventing greater violence. But the extrinsic advocate of non-violence would say this is a mistake. In the long run, violence only breeds more violence so that what may be in the short run prevent violence, is actually going to cause greater violence than if you had simply refused to use violence to defend your family and yourself.

This view is interesting because it seems to rest on a factual premise; using violence to prevent greater violence will always, in the end, cause more violence than you have prevented. However, a major problem is that it is not easy to verify such a claim. How does one go about to verify the claim? The advocate of non-violence is saying that if you had let Hitler overrun the world there would have been less violence than when nations went to war.

The problem with this is twofold: (1) The only way to find out whether this is true would have been to actually let Hitler overrun the world. But then it might have been too late to do anything, and even more important, how would you know how much violence there would have been if you had fought Hitler instead of giving in to him? In other words, it would seem that this hypothesis–that use of violence always results into greater violence–would be a very difficult factual hypothesis to verify. Another very good philosophical question is: is this hypothesis really a factual hypothesis in the first place? Or is it some disguised *a priori* judgement? We would suspect the latter, but this would be a good topic for philosophical research. If it really is a factual hypothesis, then the advocate of extrinsic non-violence would have to admit the following: that if it was clear that preventing violence by using violence would not cause greater violence, then violence would be justified–assuming that this hypothesis was truly factual, contingent and *a posteriori*. And if it were really the extrinsic one that we have described, then the formalist would have to admit that if and when this situation ever arose, then we would be justified in using violence–though he might add that such situations are extremely rare. But if he said, as we suspect he would, that there could not be such situation–where using violence would prevent more violence than it occasioned–then we would note that his hypothesis is not really a factual, contingent or *a posteriori* claim but instead an *a priori*, necessary one. And then the question would be: how does he know that this could never happen–that violence could never prevent greater violence?

(2) The second problem, with the formalist views on violence is that the same formalist kind of reasons can be given for using violence. That is, one is likely to say that some of the injustices of Hitler's regime were so bad that they should have been stopped no matter what the cost. This is not, strictly speaking, a 'problem' for the non-violence advocate, but it does show that the very same type of formalist view can be used in opposition to the formalist views on non-violence that are used in advocating the view.

But be that as it may, our interest here is simply to show that these commonly held views such as pacifism involve the arcane notions of 'right or wrong no matter what the consequences', and so, understanding these formalist concepts is necessary for understanding ideas such as pacifism.

12

Deontology or Retributivism and the Results of Punishment

We have already made it clear with respect to promising that the deontologist does not hold the view that consequences do not matter. He simply denies that consequences are the only things that count. Specifically, he says that the intrinsic nature of the action in relation to some event in the past–your having made a promise–is also relevant. The fact that you have promised to do X creates a *prima facie* obligation to do X, but does not mean that you must carry out X no matter what the consequences. The view that you must keep a promise no matter what the consequences is called the formalist view.

So there are three possible views one could hold about promising: (1) The utilitarian view that only the consequences are relevant. (2) The deontological view that though the consequences matter, the main consideration is the nature of the act, based upon past considerations. And (3) the formalist view that only the nature of the act itself matters, and that the consequences should never be taken into account.

If we posed the following question to the deontologist: Are the consequences relevant in deciding whether or not to keep a promise? The answer would be Yes and No. No, in the sense that under normal conditions, all you have to consider is the fact that you have made a promise and therefore must keep it. Yes, in the sense that under very unusual conditions, for example, someone's life or safety is in danger, the extremely bad consequences of keeping a promise may justify breaking it.

Retributivism and Recidivism

To consider this matter with respect to punishment, let us look at the concept of recidivism. This refers to the phenomenon of persons who have been sent to prison for committing more crimes, the same as or different from those that sent them to prison the first time, and being sentenced to prison again. According to criminologists, the rate of recidivism is fairly high in several countries, which means that most people released from prison, end up again in prison. So certainly the goal of deterring and correcting or rehabilitating criminals is not very successful, though this does not mean that punishment is not deterring other people because they can see what happens to those who are caught.

What is the position of the deontologist or the retributivist on recidivism? Is it of any interest to him *qua* deontologist or retributivist, or would he say that the rate of recidivism has nothing whatsoever to do with why people should be punished and is therefore of no interest to him?

Whether or not the rate of recidivism would be of interest to the deontologist or the retributivist in so far as the question of punishment is concerned, it clearly would interest him to the extent that he would accept the following observations:

(1) Other things being equal, punishment that prevents further crime is better than punishment that does not.

Therefore:

(2) Other things being equal, the lower the rate of recidivism in a penal system, the better.

The deontologist or retributivist is not unconcerned with utilitarian considerations. He naturally recognises that criminal behaviour is bad and that it is because a person has done something bad that he deserves to be punished. And so, the lower the crime rate, the better– other things being equal.

For the deontologist or retributivist, the only relevant consideration in deciding whether or not to punish someone is simply to ask: Does he deserve to be punished, that is, has he committed an act for which he deserves to be punished? If he has, then he ought to be punished; if not, then he cannot be punished. If this is so, what is the relevance of utilitarian considerations such as the likelihood of recidivism?

When we said in (1) that other things being equal, punishment that deters further crime is better than that which does not, the crucial phrase was 'other things being equal.' In this context, it means that given that the person has received as much punishment as he deserves–no more, no less–then it is better if he is deterred from further crime than if he is not. But preventing crime can never be a reason in itself for punishing a person in the first place. It can only be that he deserves to be punished because of what he has done.

Thus, the deontologist or retributivist might say that if you have to choose between two kinds of punishment–corporal punishment, say, caning and imprisonment–then other things being constant, the one that prevents crime will be better. But the *ceteris paribus* clause 'other things being equal' is crucial; in this case, it means that the two different kinds of punishment have been judged to be equally severe.

Thus, suppose someone has been convicted of assault and battery. Assume, for example, that we agree that twenty strokes of the cane plus one year in prison is equal in severity as five years in prison with no strokes, and also that the former has greater deterrent and corrective value. The deontologist or retributivist would agree that it is a preferable form of punishment, because the matter of retribution–the person getting the punishment he deserves–has already been settled and is determined to be the same in both cases. Given that the two are the same in that respect, then we are free to choose between them–and it is indeed only rational to do so–on the basis of such utilitarian considerations that are most likely to prevent further crime.

Swiftness of Punishment

Similarly, the deontologist or retributivist would not object to the swiftness of punishment being taken into account once the issue of just punishment has been settled. Thus, it is commonly accepted among criminologists and is also a matter of plain common sense that the sooner the criminal receives his punishment the more likely it is that it will serve as a deterrent. If someone commits a crime but is not punished until five years later, he is not likely to associate, in his mind, the crime with the punishment, and thus the punishment is not likely to have much effect on his future criminal behaviour. Whereas if he is punished immediately after the crime or as soon as possible, it is much more likely to be connected in his mind with the crime and therefore deter him from further criminal behaviour.

As long as the person is getting the punishment he deserves, then it is better that he be punished immediately after the crime than years later if this increases its crime-prevention value. To this the deontologist or retributivist would agree, and it does not conflict with his position.

One way of putting the deontological or retributivist position here would be to say that with respect to punishment, deontological or retributivist considerations take absolute precedence over utilitarian considerations. Only when deontological or retributivist considerations have been fully satisfied are we allowed to take utilitarian considerations into account, at which point it is perfectly rational to do so.

The 'Anything that Works' View

What the deontologist or retributivist would resolutely reject–and so would moral common sense–is a view that since the present criminal justice system is not working, as witnessed by the high rate of recidivism, the principle that should be adopted is: 'Anything that Works'. In other words, to do whatever is necessary to see that the person does not end up in prison again. If, for example, the psychologist or criminologist tells us that there is no likelihood of this person repeating this or any other crime as is usually the case with murder, then the person should be set free immediately. A person steals a loaf of bread and we discover that the only thing that will deter him is cutting off his hand, so we do that. We are informed that another person who commits the same offence needs a good meal, so that is what we give him. Another man guilty of stealing from a blind beggar is kept in solitary confinement for ten years, since is what would deter him. Another who commits the same crime needs instead a job for deterrence purposes, so we get him employed. In all these cases, the fundamental issue is not what they deserve, but what will work to deter crime.

Such a view would strike most people, including those who espouse it in their saner moments, as monstrous and bizarre. This will be discussed later under rule-utilitarianism.

Utilitarianism and Preventive Punishment

The 'Anything-that-Works' view inevitably leads to the idea of preventive punishment. If the only thing that matters is preventing crime, why not prevent it before it occurs instead of waiting until it does?

Let us begin by stating fully what the utilitarian theory of punishment amounts to. First of all, in this view, punishment has only one ultimate goal, and that is to prevent crime, which means reducing the rate of crime as much as possible. This can only be done by two related, though distinct, means: (1) deterrence, and (2) correction.

(1) We deter crimes by providing an incentive for not committing crimes. Punishment is meant to deter crime by instilling fear of punishment; a person hesitates to commit a crime because he fears being punished if caught, and (2) we 'correct' criminals by 'rehabilitating' them, that is, turning them from criminals into law-abiding citizens.

Note that persons may also be motivated to refrain from committing crimes by what psychologists would call 'positive' as well as 'negative' reinforcement. Punishment is a negative reinforcement; but as we mentioned in the case of the anything-that-works theory, we might just as well reward someone, that is, give him positive reinforcement in order to motivate him not to commit crimes in the future.

It is important to realise that these other goals–of deterrence and correction–are only intermediate goals. The ultimate goal is prevention of crime. Deterrence and correction are only important because they serve the ultimate goal of crime prevention. If someone is deterred from a crime, then that crime, which he might otherwise have committed is prevented; and if someone is corrected, then the crime(s) that he might have committed, if he had not been corrected will also have been prevented. Ultimately, it is this goal of prevention and elimination of crime that is the sole aim of the utilitarian criminologist.

There are two groups towards whom punishment is directed: (1) those who have already committed crimes and have been punished, and (2) anyone else amongst the general population who might commit a crime. Note that, with the present legal system, while both the intermediate goals of punishment (deterrence and correction) apply to the first group (those who have committed crimes), only deterrence applies to the second group (those who have not committed crimes but might). While we can deter and also correct those who are in prison, we can only deter others by instilling fear of being punished, but cannot correct them. For the utilitarian criminologist, the point is to prevent crime and to reduce the crime rate.

If, for example, we asked a utilitarian criminologist why he thinks someone ought to be punished, the answer would be that punishing him is the best means of ensuring that he does not commit another crime in the future. Whatever the crime and the punishment, the important question is: Will the punishment maximally reduce the likelihood of his committing another crime? If the answer is yes, then that punishment is deserved, and if not, then it is not.

We might again ask: "What is the relevance of the fact that the person has committed a crime? Is it, for the utilitarian criminologist of any relevance, in and of itself?" The answer would be, "No." The fact that someone has committed a crime is, for the utilitarian criminologist, only relevant because it has a bearing on the likelihood that he will commit another crime in the future.

For a utilitarian criminologist, the only relevance of the fact that a person has committed a crime, and the only reason it is of interest to him is that it is–with the present state of knowledge in criminology or psychology–the best and the only way of finding out that a person has a criminal personality and hence he/she is likely to commit more crimes. For the utilitarian criminologist, having committed a crime, is important only in so far as it is an indication or evidence of future criminal behaviour. In and of itself, it is of no interest to the utilitarian criminologist who would say "What is past is past and over and done with". All that he cares about–and all he thinks anyone should care about–is the future.

This point is extremely interesting and important for it means that if there were a better way of determining whether someone has a criminal personality and thus is likely to commit crimes, it would be preferable. The utilitarian criminologist would agree that waiting until after the person has already committed a crime is definitely an inefficient way of finding out which persons have criminal personalities.

Assume that sciences like psychology or criminology became so advanced that it could, by means of some simple tests, determine quickly, easily and accurately who had criminal personalities and hence were likely to commit criminal acts. That would certainly be a better way of determining criminal personality than the awkward and inefficient method we are stuck with at present–simply waiting to see who commits crimes and then acting to prevent more crimes. Based on the adage: "An ounce of prevention is worth a pound of cure," it is much better to stop something bad from happening before it happens rather than waiting until it happens and then doing something to stop it happening again. For example, it is better to prevent our environment from becoming polluted than wait for it to get polluted and then have to clean it up afterwards. Even if we were successful in cleaning it up, we would still have the pollution for some time, whereas if we had prevented it we would never have had pollution in the first place. Similarly, preventing a disease, say cholera, by keeping the water clean is much better than waiting till people get cholera and then try to treat them. Even if everyone is cured, which is unlikely, still many people will have had the disease for some time.

In the same way, preventing people from committing crimes is far much better than waiting till they commit them and then preventing them from committing further crimes. Our present circumstances of limited knowledge and the relatively backward state of the science of criminal psychology prevent us from determining beforehand who was likely to commit crimes. According to the utilitarian criminologist, it would be better to practice preventive punishment if we were in a position to, rather than 'curative' punishment.

Let us assume that we have a population of 100 potential criminals. If we used curative punishment, and even if our state of recidivism were 0 per cent, it would still mean that there are likely to be 100 crimes committed, whereas if we knew in advance and practised preventive punishment, there would be no crimes at all, since all 100 people would be 'punished' before they are able to commit any crimes.

The point here is that our moral common sense reacts with abhorrence to such ideas. The suggestion that people should be arrested and 'punished' even though they have not done anything wrong strikes us as quite wrong. Yet, the deontologist argues that this is what the utilitarian theory would sanction. If utilitarianism was correct, and if it was applied systematically as in the hypothetical knowledge-situation that we have described, this sort of thing would be reasonably justified.

The utilitarian may argue that while preventive punishment might deter those who were punished, it would not deter other potential criminals but would, on the contrary, encourage them. A potential criminal would reason thus:

> With this new law, which allows the government to punish you before you have even committed any crime–just because they think you are capable of committing a crime–there's no reason

why I should not rape and pillage as I've been wanting to. Because even if I don't, I'm still likely to be arrested and punished because they will know that I was going to commit a crime. So there's no reason not to.

However, in the 'old' system of 'curative' punishment, this person might have been deterred from committing these crimes because he might think: "If I commit these crimes, I may be caught and punished, but if I don't I can't be punished. So I think I'd better not".

The utilitarian would say that the utilitarian theory does not sanction preventive punishment. Hence, this argument cannot be used against the utilitarian theory.

The Deontologist's Response

There is, however, some defect in this kind of reasoning. This is because if we allow ourselves to envisage an ideal knowledge-situation *vis-à-vis* criminal psychology, then we would know, for all individuals, the likelihood of their committing crimes. Hence, we would ideally be able to prevent all crimes. Expressed differently, imagine something beyond the year 2050, where Big Brother watched everyone all the time. Add to this the idea that Big Brother also knew who was and who was not likely to commit a crime, and that all of this information was kept in a gigantic computer. As soon as anyone came into the category of 'a person likely to commit a crime within the next 24 hours,' the authorities would immediately be apprised of this fact and the person immediately arrested because they already know where everyone is at all time. We need not imagine that the police would be corrupt or cruel or anything of the sort. They would simply and honestly be doing their job of preventing crimes. We can assume that the computers and the scientific apparatus would perform flawlessly so that only those who *would* really commit crimes would be arrested and punished. The rest of us law-abiding folk would be left completely alone.

In short, in the 'ideal' situation imagined—an ideal police state—our distinction between the two groups who need to be deterred would simply cease to exist. There would not be two groups: (a) those who have committed crimes and need to be prevented from committing further crimes, and (b) those who have not committed crimes but who would if they are not deterred. There would only be one group of those who would commit crimes if not deterred by preventive punishment. Hence, there would be no crimes committed.

Thus, we do not think this attempt by the utilitarian to escape the consequences of his theory is valid. If the utilitarian theory were correct, then this ideal police state in which crime was prevented before it occurred, would be the best possible state of affairs–since that is all the utilitarian criminologist cares about; preventing crime. Our moral common sense tells us that it would be quite horrific. The injunction against punishing the innocent is one of the strongest and most absolute of all moral principles, since it involves the notion of justice. Preventive punishment violates this principle, and for that reason violates our moral common sense. Since the utilitarian theory entails that preventive punishment would be justified, yet this criticism shows that preventive punishment is not justified, this reasoning–by *modus tollens*–constitutes a strong argument against utilitarianism.

Deontological Theory of Punishment and Utilitarian Considerations

We have said that for the deontologist, there are two distinct, though related issues which must be settled entirely by deontological considerations: (1) Whether a person should be punished at all, and (2) if so, by how?

(1) If he is to be punished, it should be determined solely on the basis of whether or not he has done something which deserves punishment. A person may be punished if and only if he has done something to deserve the punishment.

(2) If a person deserves punishment, how much he should be punished depends on the nature of his crime. In general, the idea is that the punishment should fit the crime; a person should be punished as severely as is warranted by his crime. To punish him less than he deserves is like letting a guilty person go free. And to punish him more than he deserves is like punishing an innocent

person. If he deserves one year in prison and is given five, that amounts to giving him four years in prison which he does not deserve. And while it is bad to punish someone less than he deserves, it is much worse to punish someone more than he deserves. The law tries to prevent an innocent person from being punished rather than letting a guilty person go free. Similarly, most legal systems, because they are liable to mistakes, arrange things in such a way that the errors will as much as possible be on the side of a person receiving less punishment than he deserves, rather than more.

But all that the deontological considerations determine is whether one deserves to be punished, and if so, *how much*–how severely–the person ought to be punished. They do not determine *how* a person is to be punished, but to what extent a person ought to be punished. What is the difference between '*how much* a person ought to be punished' and '*how* he is to be punished'?

Every form of punishment must admit some degree in which it is of equal severity with some degree of another form of punishment. For example, however severe punishment of one year in prison is, there has to be some number of strokes of a cane that might be equal in severity to it as punishment. Similarly, one year in solitary confinement must be equal in severity to some greater length in prison under normal condition.

How different forms of punishment could be equated would be an interesting matter for behavioural scientists. Presumably, one could ask many persons who would have been subjected to various forms of punishment whether they would have preferred one year in solitary confinement or two, three, four years in normal prison; one year in normal prison or 20, 30, 40 strokes with a cane etc. One could ask such questions until he/she gets some figures that one could judge, on average, to be roughly equivalent. The point is that it would not be an impossible task to establish what amount of any given form of punishment is equivalent to in terms of any other form of punishment.

Now, for any crime of a given severity, a person deserved punishment of the corresponding severity. But there may be several different forms of punishment that are judged to be equally severe. Given that all of them are equally severe and that all are of a severity warranted by this person's crime, there will obviously be none that is best in terms of just deserts for in such a situation, the demands of justice will be satisfied equally well by any of them.

If the forms of punishment are equally severe then to determine the best among them would call for utilitarian considerations. Thus, one form of punishment would be best in terms of utilitarian criteria of recidivism and hence would be the right form of punishment, that is, the form of punishment with the best rate of recidivism would be considered the best. If, however, the two forms of punishment are judged to be equally good in terms of the rate of recidivism, we would have to decide between them on other utilitarian consideration, for example, on economic grounds; whichever is less costly would be better and therefore the thing to do.

This illustrates a general point that the case in which the only considerations are utilitarian ones, the right course of action would be the best one. If there are no deontological considerations of justices or any other past-looking obligations, the question of what we ought to do will be settled by whatever considerations remain, which in this case, would be what is best.

Thus, in the case of whether or not to allow cigarette advertising, and given that the only relevant considerations here are what will have the best consequences in the long run, the right thing to do is the best thing to do. When considering whether to allow it or prohibit it, assume that allowing cigarette advertising produces a lot of government revenue and promotes economic activity. On the other hand, it also causes a lot of illness. In this case, the right thing to do is the best thing to do.

In conclusion, the deontologist has no difficulty in dealing with utilitarian considerations of punishment. Such considerations as rate of recidivism are, to the deontologist, relevant, but only once all questions of justice have been dealt with and we are assured that the person will only be punished if he/she deserves to be. That he will receive only as much punishment as he deserves. Once these deontological considerations have been satisfied, there is no conflict in considering utilitarian considerations, or given that the deontological considerations between alternatives are equally good, deciding what to do on the basis of utilitarian considerations. Doing this is in no way incompatible with the deontological or retributivist theory of punishment.

A Problem for Deontology or Retributivism: Repeat Offenders

Whereas deontology or retributivism can deal with such utilitarian considerations as the rate of recidivism without undermining the basic theory, the matter may be different when we consider the question of repeat-offenders. Most legal systems would treat repeat-offenders more severely than first-time offenders. Someone convicted of committing a crime for the second time is treated more harshly than the first time, and more for severely for each subsequent crime.

From a deontological point of view, why should this be so? From the deontological standpoint, each time a person is found guilty of a crime, he should receive whatever punishment is warranted or deserved for his crime–no more, no less. Once he has suffered that punishment, we must consider that 'his slate is clean,' he has 'paid his debt' to the society, and in the eyes of the law–and justice–he should be treated no differently from anyone else. Given that he has been punished as he deserves, he clearly deserves no further punishment. That is why, for example, the deontologist would most strenuously object to keeping someone in prison beyond the time warranted by his crime. If he has paid his debt, he must be freed; there can be no justification for keeping him in prison, any more than there can be for keeping an innocent person there in the first place, as in the case of Dreyfus.

If this is so, then why should a person who is convicted of a crime for a second or third time be punished more severely than the first time? After all, he has been punished fully for committing the crime the first time. It is as if we are saying that when he commits it a second time, we are going to punish him both for the first time as well as the second time meaning he is being punished for the first offence all over again.

This scenario presents a difficulty for deontology or retributivism because the idea of treating a second-time offender more severely than a first-time offender is not only widely practised and accepted but it also seems to agree with moral common sense; in other words, it does seem right. For example, someone convicted of injuring someone while driving under the influence of alcohol for a third time must be or should be treated more harshly than the first time, for he simply has not learned his lesson. Yet it is not clear how deontology or retributivism can account for this. From a deontological point of view, a person should receive the punishment he deserves, and thereafter the 'slate is wiped clean.' It should not make any difference, then, whether the crime is his first, second or tenth; he should still get whatever punishment–and only that punishment–which he deserves. This seems to imply that the penalty for the second, third or fourth offences should be the same as for the first.

This argument seems to fly in the face of our moral common sense, which says that a person should be punished more severely as a repeat-offender than as a first-offender. And it seems that the only reason for this lies with utilitarian considerations that the repeat-offender is a menace to society and hence needs more severe punishment in order to protect the society. Or because he has shown himself to be incorrigible or more difficult to correct, he needs more severe punishment in order to provide a greater deterrent.

Expressed in different words, it is as if we are saying, "this person cannot be deterred from committing further crimes, nor can he be 'corrected' to become a law-abiding citizen. Therefore, he must be kept away from society. Hence, he must be put in prison indefinitely, at least until such time as he has been "corrected".

But:

> (1) if that is what we do on the basis of the fact that the offender has committed crimes repeatedly, then if we knew about his 'incorrectability' after his first crime, then we should have imprisoned him indefinitely, and

(2) if we accept as morally correct the idea that a person is found to be difficult to 'correct', he must be punished more severely. It would follow that we are accepting utilitarian considerations as taking precedence over deontological ones.

We are not punishing the repeat-offender more severely than the first offender because he deserves more from the point of view of justice; we are simply agreeing that from the point of view of justice, he does not deserve any more punishment than the first offender. After all, he has already paid for his previous offences. Yet we are also agreeing that he still ought to be punished more because that is what is needed to correct his behaviour and prevent him from doing it again. These seem to be purely utilitarian reasons, which are in this case given precedence over deontological considerations.

This kind of argument contradicts our earlier conclusion that utilitarian considerations can only be brought to bear when all deontological considerations of justice and deserts have been dealt with. In the case of repeat-offenders as opposed to first offenders, this does seem to be the case. However, in terms of justice and deserts, there seem to be no reason why the repeat-offender should be punished more severely than the first-offender. They have committed crimes of equal seriousness, and neither has a 'debt' since the repeat-offender has already paid any previous debts by being punished.

Yet our moral common sense tells us clearly that the repeat-offender should be dealt with more severely. It seems as if the only reason for this can be essentially utilitarian ones, which in this case take precedence over deontological ones. If this is true, it is the first serious fault that we have found in the Deontological Theory of Ethics. In other words, it is the first example where deontology is not in agreement with our moral common sense.

Deontological Obligations

According to the deontological or retributivist view of punishment, as well as our moral common sense, a person is punished because of what he has done. As a result of which we have an obligation to make the score even by punishing the offender: hence, the 'slate has been wiped clean', he has paid his 'debt' to society. Similar things can happen between individuals or groups of individuals outside a legal context. One person can wrong another, notwithstanding similar rights and obligations.

Civil Wrong: Torts

First there is the field of civil as opposed to criminal law, which is concerned with wrongs committed by one individual or entity against another, generally known by the term torts. These are wrongs committed by one party against another, and for a variety of reasons, do not come under the rubric of crimes. Nevertheless, for these wrongs, the law allows the wronged party to have legal recourse in the name of a civil suit.

Thus, if you wrote in the newspaper that I am a thief, thereby harming my reputation, I can sue you for defamation of my character or libel. If a civil court decides that you have defamed me, it can punish you by ordering you to pay me some sum of money. This can take two forms: (1) Compensatory–to repay actual damages done to me, e.g. loss of income. (2) Punitive damages–money which you must pay for the sake of punishing you for defaming my reputation.

The latter form–that is punitive damages–is interesting because it shows that the law itself recognises the fact that to right a wrong, it is not always sufficient merely to pay back the loss caused, but that sometimes the person must be made to suffer a loss himself because of the wrong he has committed. For if I maliciously defame you, the law does not think it is enough that I merely be made to pay you any actual loss you have suffered. Instead, I must be made to suffer an additional loss, a kind of repayment for the moral wrong that I have done, just to 'teach me a lesson.'

Extra-Legal Wrongs

Let us also consider wrongs done outside any legal context. These can occur, for example, in a segment of society that, for certain reasons, does not wish to avail itself of legal remedies or may deal with wrongs for which remedies are simply not appreciated. Thus, people who live outside the law, such as gangsters, rascals, do not often appeal to the law to right wrongs; they deal with it themselves. This however does not mean that they cannot be wronged, nor that they may not deal with them with complete justice on their side. If one person cheats another in some personal dealings, it may not be the kind of thing for which the law is an appropriate means of redress.

Consider the following example. If a man tells a woman that he will give her a job, just as a means of seducing her, and then he later disappears, that woman would justifiably feel wronged by that man and would rightly feel that she ought to revenge. Yet, it would be rather absurd to imagine that the law should intervene and have the man arrested.

Moral Debts or Claims

Moral debts or claims are relationships which one person can have in relation to another due to what has taken place in the past, just as a criminal has a debt to society and society a claim against him as a result of a crime he has committed.

There are two ways in which moral debts or claims can arise, either: (1) through positive or helpful acts, or (2) through negative or harmful acts. Generally speaking, a moral debt implies a corresponding moral claim and *vice versa*. If I am in your debt then you will have a claim against me. And if I have a claim against you that will mean that you are in my debt. But as we will see, that is not always the case.

Let us try to catalogue some of the ways that moral debts or claims can arise:

(a)   Positive moral debts or claims

These may further be divided into those, which are solicited versus those, which are unsolicited.

(i) *Solicited.* Suppose an attempt has been made on your brother's life by a rival gang. You have an old friend from that group of gangsters with 'connections,' and you ask him to intervene to help your brother. He agrees to help and succeeds in persuading the other gangsters to keep off your brother.

Clearly, you are in his debt for what he has done for you and similarly, he has a claim against you–not for a wrong you have done to him but for the good he has done for you. He has your brother's safety and this means that you owe him something. At any time in the future, if he is in need of help and asks you for it, you will have an obligation to give it to him, above and beyond whatever obligation you might have to help anyone in need of such help.

Thus, if Randie has helped get your brother out of such trouble, and that at some time later, both Randie and Brian are in need of the same kind of help–their businesses are failing and they need cash. Assume also that you are in a position to help only one of them, and that you are not indebted to Brian in any particular way–even though he might actually be a better friend of yours than Randie. You would be obliged to help Randie over Brian just because he once helped you, and not because you think he is more likely to help you in the future. On the contrary, it might well be that Brian would be a more useful person to help in the sense of getting any future benefits. Your obligation to help Randie would be based solely on the events of the past–that he helped you when you were in need and therefore you are indebted to him. This would, among other things, be a good example of a deontological obligation which the utilitarian would have great difficulty accounting for.

(ii) *Unsolicited.* Suppose that your brother's life is in danger from the gangsters and Randie intervenes without even you asking him to. The main difference between this and the previous case of solicited help is that in the case of unsolicited help, although you would be in his debt, it is not certain that he would have a claim against you. This is because if you asked for my help and got it, I could reasonably say to you at some future date: "When you asked for my help I agreed; now I need your help." Whereas if my previous help was unsolicited, it is not clear that I would be free to make such a claim against you. You may have an obligation to help me because of my previous help to you, but that does not mean that I am in a position to demand that you reciprocate. For although I did help you in the past, you did not ask for it. I simply helped without being asked. Hence, you could say to me:

> I'm sorry, I appreciate your having helped me in the past, but I never asked you to help, hence I don't think you're in a position to demand that I help you in return as you would if I had asked for your help when you gave it before.

It is like the difference between a loan and a gift. If you asked me for help, I can say "Ok, but don't forget you owe me a favour." In other words, I am making an explicit claim on you. I am helping you but I am clearly stating that I am not doing this for free, that I am expecting something in return. The understanding is that if at some time in the future I need a favour, I will feel free to ask it of you and expect to get it.

Compare this to saying, in response to your asking for help "No problem, of course I can do it, you need not worry about it. You don't owe me a thing." Now you owe him something and are in his debt; he helped you when you needed help and you would have an obligation to help him if he ever needed it. But he could not, as easily as the first person, come to you in the future more or less demanding your help. After all, he has said: "You don't owe me a thing."

In other words, a loan is something given with strings attached: I expect something back. This is how it is likely to be understood if it is solicited. A gift, on the other hand, is something done with no strings attached—you owe me nothing. This is how it is likely to be understood if it is unsolicited.

(b)   Negative moral debts or claims

The other way in which moral debts or claims can arise is by negative actions or some wrong acts. Let us distinguish between two categories of wrong actions: (i) those in which liability and responsibility for reparations are accepted by those causing the wrong, and (ii) those in which no such responsibility is accepted.

(i) *Wrong admitted responsibility*. Assume you hired someone to guard your warehouse containing bootleg whisky without telling him that it is a rather dangerous job, and while on duty he is murdered by rival gangsters who burn the building down. Although you did not cause his death, you feel or accept some responsibility for it. You did not warn him about how dangerous it was for fear he might not take the job. Were it not for this job, he would still be alive. Hence, you accept responsibility for the loss caused to his family, now without a breadwinner, and feel that you henceforth have an obligation or a debt to the man's wife and children; you employ the man's children, and send some of them to university, etc. This is a case where one person has inadvertently caused a wrong to another, but openly accepts responsibility and undertakes to repay the moral debt incurred.

We note certain things about this case:

(1) Unlike a debt arising from a positive action, this one arises, in effect, from me taking something away from you although not deliberately.

(2) Since the perpetrator of the wrong freely accepts his responsibility and expresses his willingness to make amends, there is no need for the victim to take any action against him. Though the victim might still be said to have a claim against him, the need for expressing this claim never arises since the person causing the loss pre-empts this by explicitly undertaking to repay the loss. If our cars are involved in an accident and I immediately accept the blame and agree to compensate you for any loss, there is no need for you to make a claim against me. On the other hand, if I refuse to accept responsibility, then it would be necessary for you to make a claim against me.

(3) We note that even in the case of accepted responsibility, it is not enough for the debt to be repaid so that the victim recovers his loss; what is required is that the person causing the loss assumes responsibility for the victim recovering the loss. Thus, in the bootlegger case, if after the man's death, the wife is lucky and marries a wealthy man, the perpetrator is not absolved of his obligation to right the wrong done, for he would not have been responsible for her recovering the loss. He would at least have to offer something else that could be seen as paying his debt;

and if there is nothing, then he must accept a continuing debt, which may be paid at any time in the future.

The continuing debt can manifest itself in much the same way as a debt arising from a positive action. If, at some time in the future, I am faced with the choice of helping one of two people, one of whom is the man's wife and the other is someone to whom I have no specific obligation, I would be obliged to help the former.

(4) Bear in mind that even in the case of a wrong that was deliberate, if I immediately admit liability and agree to make amends, this may pre-empt any need for the victim to make a claim against me. Conversely, if I cause a loss inadvertently but refuse to accept responsibility for it and to make good the loss, the victim would then make a claim against me. That is, the key element that distinguishes our two categories is not whether it is deliberate or accidental, rather, whether the perpetrator accepts responsibility or not.

(ii) *Wrong un-admitted responsibility.* These are wrongs for which responsibility is not accepted. They are usually deliberate, and often done from malice.

Thus, when one bootlegger burns down the other's warehouse killing people in the process, he does not undertake to make reparations for the heinous crime since the loss was caused deliberately, with malice. If he had any thoughts of making reparations he would not have caused the damage in the first place. Hence, if there is going to be any make good the losses, it will have to be done by the victim or his family.

How can the victim of such a deliberate wrong *right* the wrong? Assume that by burning down Brian's warehouse, Randie has caused Brian a loss of Kshs. 10 million. This does not mean that Randie will have benefited by Kshs. 10 million. He may but he need not. If the warehouse and all its contents were destroyed, then no one benefited from them; it was simply a colossal loss. What is important, however, is that Brian has suffered a loss of Kshs. 10 million at Randie's hands.

In the case of an inadvertently caused wrong, where the perpetrator admits responsibility and undertakes to restore the loss, the wrong can be righted by the perpetrator making good the victim's loss.

How about a deliberately caused loss for which responsibility is not accepted? The perpetrator is not going to restore the loss. If the victim is somehow able to make good all his losses, does that right the wrong? For example, if Randie destroys Brian's warehouse and a week later, just by luck–and having nothing at all to do with Randie's action–Brian finds a way of regaining his loss. He gets another even better warehouse, so that in the end, he is actually better off than he was before Randie burned down his warehouse. He has ended richer because of Randie's action. Does this *even* the score? Does it settle the claim that Brian has against Randie?

The claim is not settled because, for Brian to *even* the score, he must see to it that Randie also suffers a loss somewhat equal to his own. This is not done out of vindictiveness on Brian's part, but simply out of a sense of justice. Randie has deliberately caused Brian this loss. Brian may feel that it is only fair and just that Randie be made to pay for his crime.

There are three possibilities here:

(1) Brian recovers his loss but Randie does not suffer;
(2) Brian does not recover his loss, but Randie does suffer; and
(3) Brian recovers his loss and Randie suffers.

Of the three possibilities, presumably (3) is best because not only does Randie suffer his deserved loss, but Brian makes good his losses. The interesting question however is: which of the other two possibilities is better? Should Brian recover his loss with Randie not suffering, or should Randie suffer even though Brian does not recover his loss?

The utilitarian would say that the former is better. This is because in this case, some good comes out of it (Brian recovers his loss) and no harm is done (Randie does not suffer); while in the latter, harm is done (Randie suffers) and no good is done (Brian does not recover his loss). The latter is a complete loss, while the former is all gain. Apparently therefore, the former is better than the latter.

However, this would not be in tandem with our moral common sense because it would neither satisfy our sense of justice, nor satisfy Brian. For Brian's act of recovering his loss does not itself address the issue of justice, that is, seeing that people get what they deserve and righting the wrong that was done. Brian's recovering his loss by itself does not right the wrong that was done. This can only be done by seeing that Randie suffers, and Brian's recovering his loss has nothing to do with it. From the point of view of justice, it is much more important that the wrongdoer should suffer for his actions than that the victim recovers his loss.

Retribution, Punishment, Revenge and Retaliation or Payback Behaviour

How does the above discussion relate to the notion of punishment? One might say that what we have been talking about is revenge. Since one person causing another person harm or suffering and that person being made to suffer because of the wrong he has committed against the first person amounts to revenge.

There is a basic similarity between revenge and punishment. The former, one might say, is the natural form of something for which the latter is the legal form. Retributive punishment, is the State taking revenge for a wrong committed against a citizen, as opposed to individuals taking revenge. In terms of absolute justice, they are basically the same; both are acting on the principle that a person deserves to be made to suffer for committing crimes or wrong acts.

There are, however, some intrinsic differences. While revenge can only be carried out for a wrong done to a person, punishment can be performed for a wrong act, even if no individual is wronged. Thus, if you are convicted of being drunk while driving, even though you were not involved in an accident and did not injure anyone, you can still be punished because society considers driving while drunk a crime. But since you have not actually wronged anyone by driving while drunk, the idea of retaliation does not arise. Punishment does, of course, also apply to cases where someone is wronged; but it also applies to cases where no one is wronged but where a wrong is committed, where retaliation does not apply.

Pay-back Behaviour

A good example of natural justice might be found in payback behaviour in some traditional communities in Kenya. If someone in the neighbouring village attacks someone in another village, people in the aggrieved village would pay back the person who committed the crime. They do this because the person who committed this crime deserves to be made to suffer. This is the same underlying principle on which the retributivist theory of punishment is based; a person who commits a wrong deserves to be punished.

In some traditional Kenyan communities, it is claimed however that if you were unable to punish the actual guilty party, then you should 'punish' a relative of that person, since that will also be making the offender suffer. Would that be justified?

Assuming that the guilty man's sister had nothing whatsoever to do with the crime committed, it would be wrong to get at the offender by punishing his sister, for she is completely innocent of any wrongdoing. We have already agreed that it is always wrong to punish an innocent person. Yet, that is what we would be doing if we 'punished' the sister. If the sister is in some way responsible, even though she did not commit the crime, then that is a different story. Perhaps she might have been able to prevent it, or warn the victim, but she declined to do so.

Here we are talking about a case where she knows nothing about the crime. In that case, there can be no justification for punishing her in order to punish her brother. There is every reason to punish her brother, who actually committed the crime because he deserves to be punished, but not the sister.

We note one possible difference between punishing the guilty person only and punishing an innocent person as a way of punishing the guilty. If the guilty person alone is punished, then he and his family would have no complaints–and no moral claim–against those who paid him back. They might even apprehend the guilty person and punish him themselves, inviting the victim's family to witness it. Since the guilty person is simply getting what he deserves, there should be no ill will or grudges afterwards. A wrong has been committed and the guilty person has paid for it; that should be the end of the matter. All 'scores have been settled.'

If, however, the victim's family punishes some wholly innocent relation of the guilty man, as a means of punishing the guilty party, the result would be that the relations of the innocent person punished might very well have a complaint against those who 'punished' her, since she was not guilty of any wrongdoing. So, they will undertake to inflict their own retaliation, perhaps on entirely innocent persons, who will also feel that they have to retaliate, which can go on indefinitely. Such indiscriminate payback behaviour may well engender an unending series of such payback actions. However, payback actions directed only at those who deserve it, need not lead to an endless string of reprisals. Since the guilty party alone is punished, each side can rightly feel that justice has been done and neither side holds a grudge against the other.

Merits and Demerits of Payback

(1) *Merits*. In one sense, payback behaviour represents what we call natural justice. The principles that underlie the deontological theory of punishment are certain moral principles to the effect that when a person commits certain wrongs then he deserves to be punished. From the point of view of morality, it does not matter whether it is the state that inflicts this punishment or the victim or someone else. If anything, from the principal of justice, there is a stronger reason for the victim to inflict the punishment since he is the one who suffered the wrong. Further, it is generally agreed that the more swiftly the punishment is administered the better, in terms of prevention and deterrence. Since Western-type criminal justice systems are notoriously slow, anything else would be quicker; nothing can be quicker than punishment administered on the spot.

(2) *Demerits.* In spite of these considerations, however, there are probably stronger arguments against allowing people to administer punishment themselves. Main considerations are epistemological; that is, the problem is mainly one of knowledge. If you are absolutely certain that someone is guilty of a crime, then you would theoretically–in terms of justice and morality–be justified in inflicting the appropriate punishment on him yourself. In fact, it is better that it is done by the victim himself rather than by somebody else.

The problem, however, is that we know people often make mistakes–they are fallible–especially when acting under the influence of emotions. The desire for revenge is a very powerful emotion, which is certainly capable of clouding one's judgement.

This is not to say that the desire for revenge should be ignored. On the contrary, the desire for revenge often constitutes a very profound moral perception; that a certain person deserves to be made to suffer for what he has done. It remains a fact, however, that it often interferes with sound moral judgement.

Moreover, human beings are extremely fallible, capable of making errors with respect to moral as well as non-moral judgements. To determine that someone deserves to be punished requires two kinds of facts: (i) the moral fact that a particular wrong deserves some kind of punishment, and (ii) the non-moral or empirical fact that a person did indeed commit the crime.

The problem, then, with letting people administer punishment for crimes committed against them is that it is almost certain that if they do, many of them will make serious errors of judgement, both moral and non-moral. They will inflict the wrong degree of punishment, or even punish someone who is not guilty at all. Perhaps even when no crime has been committed, but someone is just acting on the basis of a rumour, they will act in the heat of emotion, under the influence and out of ignorance. They will make faulty inferences. They will jump to a conclusion that is not warranted by the evidence and is often false.

It is for these reasons that societies have legal systems with all the safeguards that we have mentioned. Safeguards such as:

(1) Presumption of innocence until proven guilty.
(2) Requiring proof 'beyond any shadow of doubt.'
(3) Requiring a unanimous verdict for conviction.
(4) Requiring the prosecution to reveal any foolproof evidence.
(5) Allowing the defence the right to appeal.
(6) Requiring police to inform an arrested person that he need not say anything until he has consulted with a lawyer.
(7) Not allowing hearsay evidence.

All of these have one major goal; to try to ensure that only the guilty are punished by making it as difficulty as possible to convict anyone.

It is for these reasons that we cannot allow people to administer punishment themselves; since it would mean that they are acting as judge, jury and executioner. The fact that the criminal justice systems of most of the Western World and those modelled after them are so unsatisfactory is very depressing. But to allow everyone to 'take the law into their own hands' would, in the long run, be much worse. If we are to have a society based on the rule of law, then only the state can take upon itself the responsibility of punishing the guilty. To do otherwise can only lead to chaos and anarchy.

In a society of ideally wise, rational and intelligent beings, it would be alright to allow people to enforce morality and justice as individuals; but such a society does not exist.

Mob justice

An even better illustration of the clash between theory and practice is mob justice. It is very common in some parts of Africa to see people accused of theft apprehended in the street and punished severely on the spot, not infrequently resulting in death. In terms of abstract justice, this is absolutely correct: he deserves it.

The problem is that on reflection, we know that such crowds meting mob justice often make mistakes, either by accident or design. A person is robbed in the street, turns around and sees the first person who resembles a 'rascal' and shouts 'thief' pointing at the 'rascal'. Immediately, everyone jumps on the person. A thief may himself shout 'thief' to create confusion and an opportunity to practise his craft!

We are not suggesting that this happens frequently; it may well be that in the vast majority of cases, the actual thief is caught and the punishment is justly administered. But the fact remains that if mob justice were allowed, we can be certain that many innocent people will be victims because such mobs are likely to make mistakes.

Thus, while we can say that: "Yes, if he is the thief he should be punished on the spot and severely," we also know that innocent people will suffer and that the interests of justice or utility will not be met.

Capital punishment

A further example illustrating this epistemological reasoning is illustrated by the question of capital punishment. Can a person believe, in terms of morality and justice, that one who commits murder or treason deserves to be put to death, and at the same time be against punishment? If so, how and why?

Suppose you believe that for such crimes, a person deserves without any question, to be executed. If we are absolutely certain that the person was guilty, then we would say that he ought to be executed. But human beings are fallible. It is always possible that we are making a mistake in any given case. Moreover, if capital punishment is widely practiced, then we can say that mistakes will be made, meaning that people who are innocent will be found guilty and subsequently executed.

The problem with capital punishment is that it is irrevocable; once a person is executed, he cannot be resurrected. However, if a person is put in prison and it is later discovered that a mistake was made and the person was innocent, at least he can be released and some restitution made. If he has been executed, he is dead and nothing can be done about it.

Therefore, someone can argue:

> I am against capital punishment due to some epistemological considerations—mistakes are bound to occur and innocent persons will be put to death, something that must be avoided at all costs. Therefore, we should not practice capital punishment even though on moral grounds, it is justified.

We note that these epistemological considerations apply to all kinds of punishment, not merely capital punishment. That is, we must always be concerned with, and try to prevent, miscarriages of justice—the innocent being punished wrongly. To prevent this, we have all the various safeguards—requiring proof beyond a shadow of a doubt, requiring a unanimous verdict for conviction, presumption of innocence until proven guilty, etc. This is because it is wrong to punish an innocent person, even if this means his spending only a day in prison.

Capital punishment, however, presents a special problem, because if there is miscarriage of justice, it will be irreversible, whereas with other forms of punishment, the miscarriage of justice is reversible.

This characteristic is not unique to capital punishment. Amputation of hands as practised in Islamic societies for theft is also irreversible. Though the amputee is not dead, the punishment of having his hand amputated is complete once it is done. If the person is later found innocent, the punishment cannot be rescinded. So is the case with such forms of punishment as branding which was common in European countries long ago.

Capital punishment is unique, however, in that nothing at all can be done by way of restitution. In the case of other irreversible punishments, the person could be publicly exonerated and some kind of restitution made, however inadequate. In the case of capital punishment, nothing whatsoever can be done. So of all forms of punishment, it is the one that requires the most care in administering.

13

Exceptions to Moral Principles

Apparent Exceptions: Additive Whole

One thing which has repeatedly been emphasised is that even if we accept the moral principle that it is always wrong to break a promise, there may nevertheless be cases where it is not wrong. Consider the statement:

(1) It is always wrong to break a promise, even though sometimes it is justified.

The statement can be understood in such a way that it is not a contradiction, but is in fact true. What it means is that, though it is always *prima facie* wrong to break a promise, there would be instances of breaking a promise that are resultantly right. For instance, you are on your way to keeping your promise and meeting someone in urgent need of help. You help the person but *ipso facto* do not keep your promise. Here, we say breaking your promise would be, everything considered–not wrong. Nevertheless, the element of breaking a promise is in this case still *prima facie* wrong. It is just that its *prima facie* wrongness is outweighed by the *prima facie* rightness of saving someone's life.

We note two important things here:

(i) First, what we are saying is that a *prima facie* wrong is a very different sort of thing from that which is not resultantly wrong. What we are calling *prima facie* wrong is the abstract entity, the property or characteristic (element or aspect) of promise-breaking. This must be distinguished from any specific instance of promise-breaking, that is, any particular act, which happens to involve the breaking of a promise. Any particular instance of promise-breaking is a concrete entity which occurs at some specific time and place. On the contrary, the element or property of "breaking of a promise" does not exist or occur at any particular time or space. It is something that can characterise any number of specific or concrete acts. For example, the difference between some particular car and the car's reliability: the car is at some particular place and time; but its reliability is not something that exists in any place. It can characterise an infinite number of cars all over the world. And when we say that a car's reliability is *prima facie* good even though the car is, on balance, not good, we are talking about two very different things: the property of its reliability, which is an abstract entity and the car itself, which is a concrete entity.

Thus, in the case of promising, what we are calling *prima facie* wrong is the property of promise-breaking, which is an abstract entity, not existing at any particular place or time. On the other hand, what we are saying is not resultantly wrong is this specific instance–this act of promise-breaking, which is a concrete entity occurring in a particular place and time.

(ii) The second and equally important point to note is that what we are saying about each of these two very different things–the property of promise-breaking and the specific instance of it–are also completely different. What we are saying about the property of promise-breaking is that it is *prima facie* or intrinsically wrong, nothing more. But what we are saying about the specific instance of promise-breaking is that it is not–everything considered, resultantly wrong.

Thus, there is no inconsistency between asserting:

(2) It is always *prima facie* wrong to break a promise.
And,
(3) Some instances of breaking promises are not resultantly wrong.

Thought-Experiment

One way of looking at the elements of promise-breaking as being *prima facie* wrong and not resultantly wrong is by asking ourselves what we would say if certain things were the case. This is what we will refer to as thought-experiment. That is, if we could manage to save an injured person's life without having to break the promise, that would be better. This demonstrates that as a part of the whole, taking the injured person to the hospital and thereby having to break your promise, the feature of breaking your promise still contributes *prima facie* wrongness to the whole. This is because when, in our thought-experiment, we remove that one feature, the whole gets better.

The following would be a good analogy. Suppose I own several small businesses, most of which are profitable but some are not, and I manage to get rid of the one that is losing money, my net profit will go up. And if I wanted to find out whether this particular business was making or losing money, I could experiment (though it would not be a thought-experiment) by stopping the business for sometime and seeing if the balance of profit increased. If it did, I may conclude that that business had been operating at a loss.

Additive Wholes

The reason we can evaluate our promise-breaking example using a thought-experiment is because it is what we may call the additive whole. That is, it is a whole–a particular act–whose resultant moral characteristics are the sum of the moral characteristics of the parts. An additive whole is a whole in which the moral property of the whole–its resultant goodness, rightness or wrongness–can only be determined by knowing the moral value of each of the parts, and then literally adding the moral values of the parts to get a result. For example, having to break a promise is a bad thing (-5), and saving a person's life is a good thing (+10). So, if we weigh the two together, we get a result of +5, meaning that the act as a whole is good because the good outweighs the bad.

Thus, we may conclude that the proposition:

(4) Breaking a promise to save someone's life is not wrong;

is not a genuine exception, but is only an apparent exception to the moral principle that:

(5) It is always *prima facie* wrong to break a promise;

because as far as (5) goes, we still hold that it is true without exception even though we admit that (4) is also true.

How about the proposition:

(6) It is always wrong to take human life.

Imagine someone says that this is not always true because there are cases where it is right to take human life:

(7) In a wartime situation, where a comrade is mortally wounded and you are unable to carry him, and if he is captured by the enemy he would be tortured, it would not be wrong to deliberately take his life.

Now the question: is (7) a genuine exception to (6)? It appears to be so since (6) says that it is always wrong to do a certain thing while (7) appears to point to an example where it is not wrong.

The answer is that (6) must be understood to mean something like:

(6') The aspect of 'taking a human life' is always *prima facie* wrong.

While (7) must be understood as:

(7') In a wartime situation, where a comrade is mortally wounded and you are unable to carry him and if captured he would be tortured taking his life deliberately would not be resultantly wrong.

That (7') is not compatible with (6') and, performing the following thought-experiment, we can see that in fact (6') remains true within the context of (7'):

(8) Would it be better or worse, or neither, if we could accomplish the same ends of preventing the wounded man's torture yet still not have to kill him, for example, if we could manage to take him with us if, say, we could get our vehicle running? In

other words, if we could have saved his life instead of taking it, would it be better or worse?

Obviously, it would be much better. This is because taking his life in the original situation was still *prima facie* wrong. It was only that that *prima facie* wrongness was outweighed by the stronger reason for taking his life. If you remove one bad thing from an additive whole, the whole must certainly become better. The fact that this imagined whole would be better is proof that taking his life was *prima facie* bad.

This is a perfectly good general point. With any example, we can always ask this question: Would the whole be better if the bad part were removed or lessened and, would it be worse if it were increased? If the answer is yes, then that proves that the part is *prima facie* bad.

Suppose someone asserts:

(9) Pain and suffering is always bad.

Can this be contradicted by the proposition?

(10) Having a tooth drilled by a dentist is painful but it is not bad. It is good because it saves your tooth and also saves you future pain.

Is (10) an exception to the principle asserted in (9)?

Let us perform some thought-experiment here. Would the situation described in (10) be better or worse, or neither if we could save the tooth and prevent future pain, yet have either less pain in the drilling or none at all? If everything else were to remain the same–if we would accomplish the same ends of saving the tooth–yet have less pain that would clearly be better. Having the tooth drilled and being subjected to pain is only good because its benefits outweigh the *prima facie* badness of the pain so that the event as whole becomes on balance, good. If you were to lessen the pain, the whole would become even better.

We can generalise this and argue that whether you decreased or increased the pain, the whole would become correspondingly better or worse. If you lessened the pain a little, the whole would become a little better; if you lessened it a lot, the whole would become a lot better. If, on the other hand, you increased the pain, the whole would become much worse. So, there is a point at which, if the pain and suffering became bad enough, the whole would cease to be, on balance, good. That is, while it is worth undergoing a certain amount of pain in order to save your tooth, it would not be worth it if the pain became so severe. And we would say that in that case, with such a great amount of pain and suffering, the whole would not be good.

None of the examples we have considered so far–all of which consist of additive wholes–constitute genuine exceptions to their corresponding moral principles. In all such cases, the exceptions are merely apparent.

Genuine Exceptions: Organic Whole

There are other kinds of cases that are quite different from the ones we have considered so far, which constitute genuine exceptions to these and other moral principles. In the above examples, moral principles like 'pain and suffering as always bad' can be considered universally true. That is, under all conditions, pain and suffering are always *prima facie* bad.

Let us consider the pain and suffering of someone who is being deservedly punished. Such an event or whole, of the person being punished for some crime he has committed, clearly contains pain and suffering as a part, and if he deserves this suffering (say, ten strokes of a cane), then the event of his being punished and experiencing this suffering is good.

How about the pain and suffering itself? The fact that the whole, of which this pain and suffering is merely a part, is good does not mean that the pain and suffering is in itself good. As we have observed with the tooth-drilling example, the pain from the drilled tooth is considered bad even though the whole is good. For though the whole is good, the pain itself is still bad.

So, the fact that punishing someone is good, even though it involves pain and suffering, is not enough for us to say that the pain and suffering is good; it may still itself be bad even though the whole is good.

Now, how about the man who deserves ten strokes of the cane? If his suffering were still in and of itself bad (and on the whole resultantly good), then if we lessened the pain and suffering or removed it altogether, that should make the whole better. But the crucial question is; does it? That is, if we think this person deserves ten strokes, would it be better if we gave him only two strokes instead? Clearly, if we think he deserves ten strokes, then it would not be good to give him fewer strokes; it would be worse. If he deserves ten strokes and he gets less, he would not be getting the punishment he deserves. If we gave him none, he would not be punished at all. And if he deserves to be punished, to punish him less than he deserves or not would in itself be bad.

However, if the pain and suffering in this case was in and of itself bad, then lessening it would make the whole better. However, in this particular case, it does not make the whole better and we can therefore conclude that the pain and suffering of punishment is not, in and of itself, bad.

We note, again, the *modus tollens* reasoning being used here:
(11) If the pain and suffering of punishment was in itself bad, then lessening that pain would make the whole better.
(12) But lessening the pain and suffering does not make the whole better; it makes it worse.
(13) Therefore: The pain and suffering of punishment is not in itself bad.

If we cannot say that the pain and suffering of punishment is in itself bad, then can we say that it is good?

To answer this question, we can use another thought-experiment. That is, if the pain and suffering of punishment were in itself good, then if we increased it, the whole should get better, and generally, the more pain the better. If the person deserves ten strokes of the cane, would it be better if he got 15 instead, and even better if he got

20? If he deserved 10 and got none, it would be worse. So if he got two it would be better than none, for though he still would not be getting what he deserves (10), he would be getting something which is better than nothing. So, four would be better than two, six better than four, and so on, up till 10. Up to 10, the more he gets the better. For him to get more than 10 would not be better than getting a flat 10. It would be worse. This is because, if he deserves 10, then to get more than 10 is for him to get more punishment than he deserves.

Therefore, we cannot say that the pain and suffering of punishment is either *prima facie* bad or that it is *prima facie* good. What we can say is that the whole of which the punishment is a part is not an additive whole, that is, a whole whose moral properties, good or bad, right or wrong can be determined by the moral properties of each of its parts. In an additive whole you can only determine the moral characteristics of each of the parts, and then weigh them all together. An additive whole, therefore, is a whole whose moral quality is the sum of the moral qualities of all its parts.

In the case of deserved punishment, the situation is fundamentally different. We cannot determine the moral characteristics of the whole by considering those parts of the original crime, which involved certain suffering plus the suffering of the criminal being punished. For in this case, the relationship between these two parts is itself morally relevant. This is not a matter of so much suffering here or avoidance of suffering there as in the case of the tooth-drilling. Here, we have to consider not only the fact that the criminal is suffering, but that he is suffering as punishment for what he has done. In other words, we can only evaluate his suffering by considering it in relation to some event in the past, namely, his previous criminal acts.

The whole–the crime plus the criminal being punished–is an organic whole, whose moral characteristics are not just the sum of the moral characteristics of its parts. In this case–someone being punished for what he has done–the whole, consisting of his crime plus his punishment can only be judged, morally, as a whole. It cannot be judged by first judging its parts and then adding them together. This is because in the case of an organic whole, it is not only the parts that are relevant, but the parts in a certain relationship.

Thus, if Randie gets involved in a road accident and is badly injured and in great pain then that in itself is bad. Imagine, then, that Brian is also involved in a separate accident though of the same magnitude. If each of these cases is bad, say -10, then together they are add up to -20, i.e. the two accidents are clearly worse than one.

Let us assume also that Randie's accident was actually caused by Brian and that Randie had discovered that Brian has been supplying substandard spare parts for public service vehicles. As a result, several road accidents have occurred in which many commuters have lost their lives. Due to Randie's knowledge of what he has been doing, Brian tried to silence him by knocking his car off the road. Brian, in trying to get away, has also had an accident and is also writhing in great pain.

When we think of these two people suffering great pain and are no aware that there is a particular relation between the two accidents, we can say that each of them was bad and together worse than each by itself. But if we are aware that there was a relationship–we would say that Brian deserved what happened to him because of what he had done to Randie. We would not say anymore that Brian's suffering was bad. Rather, we would see it in relation to his crime and would argue that it is not bad. However, the whole, of which it is a part, becomes better by the addition of this part, even though the part if it did not have this relation to the previous event, would be bad. Added to this organic whole, it improves the whole, that is, it turns what was previous a bad situation, Randie's being nearly killed, into something less bad by adding someone's suffering because that suffering was deserved.

We note one interesting point here. Someone's suffering does not have to be deliberately inflicted by another with the purpose of punishing the person. It can as well come about by way of an accident and still be deserved suffering. What is essential, however, is that the person should deserve the suffering. This is based solely on some event in the past.

What then can we say of cases such as deserved suffering, if we cannot say that the suffering is intrinsically good or bad? In terms of such organic wholes, we cannot really assess the parts at all; we can only make a judgement of the organic whole as a unit. In the case of an additive whole, we can morally assess each of the parts in order to assess the whole. If you break a promise, the only way we can decide whether it is right or wrong is by considering each element of your action, giving it some moral weight and then adding them all together. In the case of an organic whole–such as a person receiving deserved suffering–the smallest unit that can be morally judged, or that has any moral quality, is the whole itself. Thus, it is not that the deserved suffering is in and of itself good or bad. This is because no part of the organic whole can be assessed by itself. Only the whole itself can be morally assessed.

Hence, there is a sense in which organic wholes can be said to be more–or other–than the sum of their parts. For even though each of the parts of an organic whole are things which, if they could be assessed by themselves–that is, if they were parts of additives wholes–would be bad, when they are part of an organic whole, having the relationship such as we have described, the whole is good.

Pleasure and Happiness are Good

Corresponding to the principle that pain and suffering are bad is the principle that:

(14) Pleasure and happiness are always good.

Again, we can give examples that appear to contradict this. Thus:

(15) Taking drugs, which can be very pleasurable, can nevertheless be very bad.

Thus, using a drug like heroine is highly pleasurable, but it is very bad. This does not mean that the pleasure itself is bad. The act, taken as a whole, together with all its consequences, is bad because it leads to physical addiction with the extremely undesirable consequences that go with it.

To conclude that the pleasure, as part of the whole, is still, in and of itself, *prima facie* good, we need only ask the following question: What would we say if one derived this pleasure from drugs without any of the undesirable consequences? That is, it did not create addiction and it did not keep him from work. Would it not be good or better?

Conversely, we can also ask: If the pleasure derived from the drug was much reduced or removed altogether, would it be good or bad? This would make its use much worse. Actually, there would be no reason to use it in the first place.

Similar remarks could be made about the pleasures derived from taking alcohol: The habit of taking alcohol is bad, even though it is pleasurable. But this does not mean that the pleasure, in and of itself, is bad; it only means that such actions taken as whole, and including all of the bad consequences–hangover, money spent, drunken behaviour, violence–are bad. On the other hand, if one did not derive any pleasure out of it, it would even be worse. However, if one could imagine a situation where he could get all the pleasure of drinking without any of the bad consequences, it would certainly be much better.

The above examples are all additive wholes; whereby, one part may be good (the pleasure), but another part (the consequences) bad, and the badness of the consequences may outweigh the goodness, so that the additive whole is, on balance, bad. If we could just get the pleasure of drinking without the hangover, alcoholism, addiction, etc., we might say that drinking was, on balance, good, or better than drinking with all the bad consequences. Hence, such examples do not constitute genuine exceptions to the principle that pleasure and happiness are always *prima facie* good; we can consistently maintain this principle in the face of such examples.

There are other cases that are different. Let us assume Randie and Brian have been rivals for a long time, and Brian is by far more successful. Suddenly, Brian suffers a series of disasters; thieves murder his wife and children; his business goes bankrupt, etc. Suppose Randie enjoys seeing Brian suffer in this way, that is,

Brian's misery gives Randie pleasure and happiness. How would we view Randie's happiness? Is it, in and of itself, good? Most persons, considering this case concretely, would say that his happiness was not good.

We are not saying that Randie's happiness has in any way caused Brian's unhappiness. As far as the two states of affairs are concerned, there need be no causal connection between them. Yet, we would agree that Randie's happiness is not good in this case.

To understand this, argument, we must consider the whole of which Randie's happiness is a part. We can write this as:

(16) Hr(+5) because he believes that Ub(-10),

where this can be read as: 'Randie is happy (+5) because he believes that Brian is unhappy (-10).'

Randie is happy (+5) because Brian is unhappy (-10). One may say that this is a morally undesirable state of affairs. But is this because, as we have set it up, there is a balance of unhappiness (-10) over happiness (+5)? If Randie's happiness were in itself good but was outweighed by Brian's unhappiness, then if we were to increase Randie's happiness (say to +15), thus giving us:

(17) Hr(+15) because he believes that Ub(-10),

would it make things better or worse? That is, is the situation in (17) better or worse than in (16)? Again, we would say that (17) was worse than (16), even though (17) clearly has a greater balance of happiness over unhappiness, +5 versus -5. If we were to look at these as additive wholes, and weigh the happiness against the unhappiness contained in each, we would say that (17) was not only better than (16), but (16) was also itself bad. If situations like these were additive wholes, then increasing the amount of happiness in them, everything else remaining the same, would have to make them, on balance, better. Yet as we can see (17), which differs from (16) only that Randie is even happier in (17) than in (16) is not better, but rather worse, than (16).

This is because these examples are not additive wholes but organic wholes. The moral quality of the whole is not determined simply by the moral qualities of the parts, but rather by their parts and their relationships to each other. Randie's happiness cannot be considered in isolation from its context. It can only be judged in relation to another part of the whole, that is, he is happy because Brian is unhappy. In such a relationship, we would say that his happiness is not, in and of itself, good; rather, we would say that it is bad.

Imagine, however, that instead of being happy at Brian's misfortune, Randie instead felt sympathy as a result of Brian's misfortune, thus:

(18) Ur(-10) because he believes that Ub(-10).

What would we say of this? In terms of a balance of happiness or unhappiness, (18) contains more unhappiness than either (16) or (17) [-20, compared to -5 and +5]. In this case, would we say that (18) is a morally worse–more undesirable–situation than (16) or (17)? On the contrary, we would agree that it was morally better because human sympathy would be regarded as a morally desirable trait. It is better that a person should be sympathetic to another's misfortune than being happy or even indifferent.

Consider the following three possible cases:

		taken as additive whole	taken as organic whole	actual moral common sense
18.	Ur(-10) because Ub(-10)	(-20) worst	Best	best
19.	Ir(0) because Ub(-10)	(-10) better	Worse	worse
20.	Hr(+5) because Ub(-10)	(-5) best	Worst	worst

[I = indifferent]

Here are three cases in which Randie perceives Brian's misfortune. In the first case, he is unhappy because of Brian's misfortune; in the second, he is indifferent, and in the third, he is happy. Viewed as an additive whole, they can be arranged in order of increasing balance of happiness and unhappiness (-20, -10, -5), and in an order of increasing goodness: (18) would be bad, (19) better, and (20) the best. Their actual order would be just the opposite for according to our common moral judgement, for a person to be completely indifferent to another's suffering (19), or have no sympathy thereby having no inclination to help, is very bad thing. If that is bad, it is even worse for a person to positively enjoy another's suffering as in (20). The best of the lot is the one with the least amount of happiness, that is, (18), where Randie is actually unhappy at Brian's misfortune.

Hence, all of these must be viewed as organic wholes illustrating the idea that there are wholes, which are different from the sum of their parts. The 'sum' of (18) is clearly negative–more unhappiness than happiness; in fact, it contains only unhappiness. Taken as an organic whole, however, it is better than (20) where Randie's happiness–because of Brian's misfortune–is even greater than Brian's.

In order to see how crucial the relations between the parts of these wholes are, let us assume that we change (20) in the following way: That Brian has suffered a series of misfortunes and is unhappy (-10), and that Randie is happy (+15), but that Randie's happiness is in no way related to Brian's unhappiness. We could write this as:

(21) Hr(+15) coincident but unrelated Ub(-10).

Taken as an additive whole, it would be +5. Similarly, the actual result would also be +5. In this case, there would be no reason for saying that the 'whole'–the combination of Randie's happiness and Brian's unhappiness–was bad. If we consider it as a whole, say because they were part of the same family, then we can say that though there was some unhappiness in it, the happiness–Randie's good fortune–outweighed the unhappiness, Brian's misfortune. As a result, we can say that on balance, this family was happy, that it was, everything considered, good.

In a situation like (20) the case was different. In such a situation, the happiness of one was related in a morally relevant way to the unhappiness of another. Either one was happy because he knew that the other was unhappy, or that his happiness was achieved at the other's unhappiness. Here, even though the amounts of happiness versus unhappiness were identical, the *whole* would be bad. Yet the only difference between the two is that in one (20), the parts have a morally relevant relation to each other, while in (21) they are not. In other words, in one they constitute an organic whole, and in the other an additive whole.

We have already considered apparent exceptions to the moral principle:

(6) It is always wrong to take human life.

Let us now consider what would constitute genuine exceptions to the principle.

Would euthanasia, for example, if we think it was justified, constitute a genuine exception to this principle? It wouldn't be because taking away someone's life in order to prevent suffering and to avoid expenses is still, in and of itself, *prima facie,* wrong. This can be confirmed by the same kind of thought-experiment: If we could avoid all the needless suffering and expense and still save the person's life, would it be better or worse? It would certainly be better. Therefore, we can conclude that it is only because the dreadful consequence of keeping the person alive outweighs the *prima facie* wrongness of taking the person's life, that such an act of euthanasia is, everything considered, not wrong.

Let us also consider capital punishment? We always believe that a person who has committed murder deserves to die, and that his execution is therefore good. Is this a case of saying that the execution is resultantly good because of its good consequences, while the termination of the person's life is still in itself bad? Let us rephrase the question: If we could accomplish the same ends, presumably the utilitarian ones of deterrence, without executing this man, would that be better or not? If we accept the retributive view of punishment–that capital punishment is sometimes deserved–then it would certainly not be better if he is not executed. If an execution were what he deserves, then it would be wrong to let him go unpunished or even to get less punishment than is necessary.

In short, if one accepts capital punishment as a form of punishment, which is sometimes deserved, then in such cases, it is not *prima facie* wrong to take away human life. For in cases of just executions, the taking of life would be part of an organic whole, which as an organic whole, is good. To remove that part or lessen it would make the whole worse, not better.

The important point, then, is to distinguish capital punishment from the previously discussed cases like euthanasia or the battlefield situation, which are highly apparent exceptions: capital punishment is a genuine exception. Given that you accept capital punishment as just and right, you can no longer hold that it is always *prima facie* wrong to take away human life since in a case of capital punishment, it is not *prima facie* wrong.

Conclusion

What general moral statements can we make about pain, and suffering, taking away of human life that cannot be said, in a blanket manner to be always *prima facie* bad? We cannot say, for example, that pain and suffering are always *prima facie* bad. This is so because the above examples of organic wholes are genuine exceptions to the idea that pain and suffering are always *prima facie* bad. When it is deserved, pain and suffering are not *prima facie* bad.

What general statement can we then make about the moral status of pain? When pain is part of an additive whole–when it exists in circumstances in which it can be evaluated by itself–it is always *prima facie* bad. So it is true that we cannot say that pain is always *prima facie* bad because pain does not always occur in situations where it can be assessed by itself–as part of an additive whole. It is often part of an organic whole, for instance, whenever someone who deserves to suffer, actually suffers. However, as a general statement, we can say that when it is part of an additive whole, and can be morally assessed by itself, it is always *prima facie* bad.

The same can be said of taking away human life or pleasure. When taking away human life occurs in a situation where it can be assessed by itself, for example, in the wartime situation where it is part of an additive whole it is always *prima facie* wrong. However, there are situations, for instance, the execution of a person, when the taking of a human life cannot be evaluated on its own. In such situations, it can only be judged in relation to other parts of the whole.

Part 3
Rule-Utilitarianism and The Generalisation Argument

14

The Generalisation Argument

Before discussing the third major ethical theory of generalisation argument, rule-utilitarianism, let us summarise utilitarianism or teleology and deontology. We have so far considered these two ethical theories as fundamentally different and in some kind of opposition with each other, despite the fact that each of them claims to account for all our common sense moral judgements.

Utilitarianism

(i)   *Strengths*. The strengths of utilitarianism are:

(1) It is simple–that is, it is based upon a moral principle that apparently accounts for and explains all of our common sense moral judgements. This is the principle that one should always and only do the highest good (the basic teleological principle). (2) As a result of being based on this seemingly self-evident moral principle, utilitarianism seems to provide a powerful argument to explain why whatever is right or wrong is so. It is wrong to break a promise, tell a lie, and cheat someone because doing so will, in the long run, do more harm than good.

(ii)   *Weaknesses*. Utilitarianism's basic weakness is that it cannot account for our common sense moral judgements. If the basic teleological principle (BTP) were true, and our only ultimate, intrinsic obligation were to do only what is good, then we would have no obligation to keep a death-bed promise. Actually, there would be no such thing as promising. We would be justified in keeping an innocent person in prison. We would be justified in practising preventive punishment if doing so would prevent crime. In other words, we reason by *modus tollens:*

(1) If utilitarianism were correct, there would be no such thing as promising and preventive punishment would also be justified.
(2) But preventive punishment is not justified and there is something called promising.
(3) Therefore, utilitarianism is not correct.

Deontology

(i)   *Strengths.* Deontology is strong in those respects in which utilitarianism is weak. It accounts for the judgements of our moral common sense, the only possible exception being the punishment of repeat-offenders. It correctly articulates our moral common sense by asserting that we have an obligation to keep promises, or tell the truth. It is independent of any consideration of the consequences.

(ii)   *Weaknesses.* Its main weakness lies in the areas in which utilitarianism is strong. When you ask the deontologist for an argument as to why it is *prima facie* wrong to break a promise or to tell a lie, the best answer he can give would be that 'intuition' says so. In other words, if you think about them you will 'see' that it is wrong to break a promise, to tell a lie, etc. For the deontologist, each and every moral judgement has a separate and distinct 'intuition' by which we are supposed to intuit a distinct and ultimate moral fact. He would argue that it is intrinsically wrong to break a promise, intrinsically wrong to lie, intrinsically wrong to steal, and intrinsically wrong to keep an innocent person in prison, etc.

This resort to intuiting ultimate moral judgements is not really an argument at all. When you ask a deontologist why it is wrong to keep an innocent person in prison, he would simply say 'it is wrong because it is wrong.' The implication being that there is no answer to that question, and you should not even ask it in the first place. Philosophically speaking, there is something inappropriate about such a position. Asking this question assumes that whoever is asking the question needs an answer and what the deontologist or intuitionist really wants to say is that it does not need any answer, since the truth of moral judgements is ultimately self-evident.

This answer is unsatisfactory in so far as we insist that there should be an answer to the question. Why is it wrong to break a promise or keep an innocent person in prison? The deontologist does not attempt to answer such questions, any more than saying that they should not be asked in the first place.

It is precisely because of the deontological problem discussed above that the third major ethical theory, rule-utilitarianism, comes in and claims to provide an answer. It presents an argument which shows precisely why the things which the deontological theory and our moral common sense agree are wrong.

As a basis for understanding rule-utilitarianism, let us first consider what is called the generalisation argument, since rule-utilitarianism is closely related to the generalisation argument.

Several preliminary points are worth making: (1) The generalisation argument is part of common sense; it is an argument that the ordinary person without any 'training' in philosophy or any other academic discipline or even an illiterate person will understand as a good argument and may even use on his own in appropriate circumstances. It would be of philosophical interest if one could do some research to confirm that uneducated people recognise this as a good argument and often uses it on their own. It is therefore not an argument that was created or discovered by philosophers; the philosopher's job is merely to analyse and refine it. (2) Not only does this argument exist in common sense and is considered a good argument, it is in fact a good argument and we shall take it as a philosophical datum that it is so. (3) The task of the philosopher then is not to determine whether it is a good argument, but to find out exactly why and how it is a good argument.

An Example of the Generalisation Argument?

The generalisation argument arises where one person is engaging in some behaviour, which another person thinks is wrong. Imagine that in some community there has been a serious drought and people have been asked to conserve water and use it only for essential purposes. Randie happens to visit Brian and finds him watering his lawn, and asks him:

(1) Hey, how can you water your lawn like this, don't you know there is a serious water shortage?

To which Brian replies:

(2) So what? Why shouldn't I water my lawn?

Now the situation here is that Randie is actually telling Brian that it is wrong for him to be watering his lawn when there is a water shortage. Brian's reply to this question amounts to denying that what he is doing is wrong and challenges Randie to tell him why he thinks it is wrong.

At this point, we can note the following: Randie recognises as a matter of moral common sense, that what Brian is doing is wrong. The question is: How is he likely to respond to Brian's challenge for an explanation for why it is wrong, that is, for a specific moral argument to bolster his common sense claim that watering the lawn during a drought is wrong?

We need to pay careful attention to each of the responses that Randie is likely to give to Brian's challenge. Each of the views that we will consider would be obtained from various responses indicating that not only Randie's position is part of moral common sense, but that each of the attempts to buttress this position are also part of common sense.

The first attempt to defend the claim that using water during a shortage is wrong: an act-utilitarian argument.

The first reply to this challenge is likely to be that misusing water when there is scarcity actually harms other individuals and the community thus contributing to the shortage of water.

The first thing to point out with regard to this response is that it is utilitarian, in that it appeals to the actual consequences of individual action; watering your lawn, by itself, will directly contribute to making the water shortage worse. It is therefore what we will call an act-utilitarian (as opposed to rule-utilitarian) argument, because it appeals to the consequences of the individual action.

The problem with this argument is that it is extremely weak. Unless the community and the *total* amount of water involved is very small, the amount of actual damage done by somebody watering his lawn, is bound to be so small as to be almost negligible. For example, let us suppose that we are talking about a populous city of about 10 million residents. Let us say that in watering my lawn I use 10 litres of water. This means that I am depriving everyone in that city of 0.000001 or 10 over 10,000,000 litres of water. In other words, everyone in that city will have one over one million litres less water than they could have had if I had not watered my lawn. This is assuming that my 10 litres were to be distributed evenly amongst the 10 million residents. Or, with reference to the reservoir: If the reservoir would have contained 100 million litres, it will now contain 99,999,990 litres instead.

But for practical as well as our purposes, these are quantities that are negligible–almost non existent. If you were going to base your claim that it is wrong for me to water my lawn on the consequences of this action, then your argument would be so weak that we can virtually ignore it. In fact, I could argue that watering my lawn has no measurable consequences. I could also claim that it has significant good consequences; it will benefit my family and me without harming anyone.

So we can conclude that this first attempt to defend Randie's original moral claim that watering the lawn during a water shortage is wrong fails. Though our moral position may be correct, it is not to be understood as the act-utilitarian argument that the action will itself have harmful consequences.

Applying the generalisation argument: 'Suppose everyone did that?'

Once it is realised that this simple act-utilitarian argument is inadequate to justify our common sense moral claim, we are likely to get the response "but suppose everyone did that?" Again, one of the most interesting points here is that this is an argument that most people will come up with on their own, which they will recognise, intuitively, as a good and relevant argument. It is therefore not a philosopher's argument, but one which most people would use in such a situation as a matter of common sense.

Not only would most people come up with this argument on their own and consider it a good argument, but it should also be accepted as a good argument. In fact, it can be taken as a philosophical datum, that is, something which we recognise and accept as true such that if and when any other argument or conclusion comes into conflict with it, that by itself is sufficient ground for rejecting that argument or conclusion. Thus, if we are asking whether a certain interpretation of 'suppose everyone did that' is correct–call it x–and find that it conflicts with 'suppose everyone did that'–philosophical datum–then that by itself would be sufficient to show that the interpretation (x) cannot be correct. This can be shown to be so using *modus tollens* as follows:

(3) If an interpretation of 'suppose everyone did that' (call it 'x') were correct, then 'suppose everyone did that' would not be a good argument.

(4) But we know that 'suppose everyone did that' is a good argument because it has been taken as a philosophical datum.

Therefore, 'x' cannot be a correct interpretation of 'suppose everyone did that.'

First Interpretation of the Generalisation Argument

Let us call this question 'suppose everyone did that?' a proto-generalisation argument, meaning that it is the beginning of a generalisation argument, though in a very nascent form. Our concern is not to determine whether it is a good argument–we have already agreed that it is–but to find out what it means.

The question "What if everyone did that?" or alternatively expressed as 'suppose everyone did that?' is clearly rhetorical, that is, it presupposes a certain answer, that if everyone did that it would be disastrous. Let us for the time being call this question the generalisation question, and the answer to it the generalisation premise:

(5) If everyone used water non-essentially during a drought, it would be disastrous.

So, when we ask the generalisation question it in effect contains its own answer; that is, 'if everyone did that it would be very bad.' And since anything that is very bad is presumed to be wrong, your action is bad because it is somehow connected with the fact that if everyone did as you are doing, it would have bad and unacceptable consequences.

So far, how do we understand 'suppose everyone did it?' We take it to mean that if you did something, then others will also follow suit. That is, we are taking 'suppose everyone did it' to mean that watering your lawn will cause others to do the same. And if others did so, it would be very bad and therefore wrong. Therefore, your doing it is wrong. We could express this as follows:

(6) If you use water non-essentially it will cause others to do the same.

(7) If others do this, it would have disastrous consequences.

(8) Therefore, your using water non-essentially is wrong because it will have disastrous consequences.

Let us refer to this as the first interpretation of '*suppose everyone did it*' and abbreviate it as SEDT-1.

At this juncture, the important question to ask is: is this the generalisation argument? That is, is SEDT-1 a correct interpretation of 'suppose everyone did it?' Remember that we have accepted, as a philosophical datum, that the generalisation argument represented by the common sense question 'suppose everyone did that,' is a good argument. One simple way, therefore, of deciding whether it is a correct interpretation of 'suppose everyone did that' is to ask whether SEDT-1 is a good argument. For if SEDT-1 were a correct interpretation of 'suppose everyone did that' then it would have to be a good argument, since 'suppose everyone did that' is a good argument. If, on the other hand, SEDT-1 is not a good argument, then by *modus tollens* we can infer that SEDT-1 is not a correct interpretation of 'suppose everyone did that.' Thus, if we find out that SEDT-1 is not a good argument, we can reason as follows:

> (9) If SEDT-1 is the correct interpretation of 'suppose everyone did that' then since the latter is a good argument, the former must also be a good argument.
>
> (10) But SEDT-1 is not a good argument.
>
> (11) Therefore, SEDT-1 is not the correct interpretation of 'suppose everyone did that.'

Is the argument expressed by SEDT-1 a good argument? It says, in effect, that it is wrong for one to use water wastefully during a shortage because doing so would cause others to do the same and this would have very bad consequences. Assume that Randie puts forward this argument (SEDT-1) and Brian presents the following rebuttal:

> (12) But no one else is going to follow my example because no one else will know what I'm doing. I have a very high fence around my house and I let no one in. Therefore, my watering the lawn is not going to cause anyone else to do the same, let alone everyone else.

Would this successfully rebut SEDT-1? That is, if (12) were correct, would this show that SEDT-1 is not a good argument? The answer is, Yes. SEDT-1 interprets 'suppose everyone did that' as asserting that it is wrong to water your lawn during a shortage because doing so will cause others to do the same. This in effect is just another variant of the first interpretation of the generalisation argument, that using water non-essentially will itself harm others. It is only that instead of saying that you will harm others directly by depriving them of water; it says that you will indirectly harm others by causing people to use water wastefully and thereby harm others.

In order to refute this argument, all that needs to be done is to show that the action will not cause others to do the same. And you can do so by demonstrating that no one else will know what you are doing so that you cannot possibly influence them in that respect.

Brian could continue as follows:

(13) My using water in this way cannot possibly make any difference. Why? Well, either enough people are going to conserve water or they are not. If enough people do, then my using 10 or 100 or even 1,000 litres extra is not going to do any harm given that we're talking about hundreds of millions of litres. At any rate, it won't matter if instead of 100,000,000 litres, there are only 99,999,900. For if the former amount will be enough, then so will the latter; if the latter is not enough, then neither will the former.

If, on the other hand, most people are not going to conserve water, so that the level in the reservoir goes down to 20,000,000 litres and there is a disaster, my conserving or not conserving would not matter. Indeed, it wouldn't have helped things if instead of 20,000,000 litres there were instead 20,000,100 because I didn't water my lawn.

In short, whatever I do will make no difference. My conserving water will help no one and my using it will harm no one. On the contrary, my not using it will harm my family and me and using it will be of benefit to me and my family and those who would have failed to conserve.

This is a very important conclusion. It establishes clearly that my using water during the shortage will harm no one but will actually benefit several people.

Therefore, if SEDT-1 were a correct interpretation of 'suppose everyone did that,' we could then say that 'suppose everyone did that' was not a good argument because this rebuttal of SEDT-1 [contained in (12) together with (13)] would also then successfully rebut 'suppose everyone did that.' But we have already agreed that 'suppose everyone did that' is a good argument. Therefore we can say that SEDT-1 is not a correct interpretation of 'suppose everyone did that.' In other words, by *modus tollens:*

(14) If 'suppose everyone did that' meant SEDT-1, that is, it were a correct interpretation of 'suppose everyone did that,' then it could be refuted by 12 and 13.

(15) But 'suppose everyone did that' is not refuted by 12 and 13, that in spite of these two statements being true, we nevertheless accept 'suppose everyone did that' as a good argument.

(16) Therefore, SEDT-1 is not the correct interpretation of 'suppose everyone did that.'

The Correct Interpretation of the Generalisation Argument

If 'suppose everyone did that'–the generalisation argument–does not mean that if you do this others will, what does it mean? It is clear that the generalisation argument is asserting some connection between your using water in a wasteful manner and everyone's doing so. If the connection between your action and those of others is not causal, what is it?

To answer this question, we must go back to the beginning of the argument. The argument started with a moral disagreement: *I saw you watering your lawn during a shortage and said it was wrong.* You challenged me by asking why it is wrong. You wanted to know why. By asking that question, you were clearly expressing your disagreement with what I had said, that is, you were saying that your action was not wrong and that I was not right in saying that it was wrong. Hence, you were clearly taking a moral position and making a moral judgement.

Supervenience and Universality

Here, we must recall two very important concepts from our earlier discussion, namely: *supervenience* and *universality*. Moral judgements are supervenient; that is, whenever we say that something is right, wrong, good or bad, there must be some feature(s) of the action, person or state of affairs by virtue of which it is considered right, wrong, good or bad.

Thus, if you say that it is not wrong for you to use water non-essentially during a shortage, one can ask: "Why? Under what circumstances are you justified in doing this?" And you must be able to cite these features. In our case, you would say that your using the water will harm no one and will actually benefit a few people. So you are saying that it is alright for you to use the water in this way because your doing so will do more good than harm.

However, we may ask, if it is alright for you to do this, isn't it also right for anyone in the same situation to do it? We are not saying that they will do it; we accept your statement that no one else will know that you are doing it and that your action will not influence anyone else. What we are asking is this. If what you are saying were true, that it is okay for you to use the water because it will do more good than harm, then must it not follow that it will be okay for anyone and everyone else to do so? For this simply expresses the universality of moral judgements, which in turn is based upon their supervenience. If certain facts make one action right, then they *ipso facto* and necessarily make any action with the same features equally right. Therefore, if one action–yours–is right because it will do more good than harm, then any such action performed anywhere by anyone, at any time, must be equally right.

For example, it would be quite absurd for someone to say; 'It is okay for me to use water in a non-essential because it will do more good than harm, but it would not be alright for you to do the very same thing–because you are *you* and I am *me*! Or because I am here and you are there.' This would be as absurd as saying: 'It is okay for me but not for you because my name is Randie and yours is Brian!' There may be special circumstances that would justify my doing it and your not doing it; but my being here or being named Randie and your being there or being named Brian are not such special circumstances.

Hence, we can conclude: If you claim to be justified in using water non-essentially during a drought for these reasons, then you are *ipso facto* saying that it would be equally right for anyone to do likewise. But based on the generalisation premise, you have already admitted that it would not be right for everyone to do this since we have already agreed that:

(17) If everyone used water in a wasteful way during a drought, it would be a disaster.

But if it is not okay for everyone, then, by *modus tollens*, it cannot be so for you. The whole argument can then be expressed as follows:

(18) If it is right for you to use water non-essentially during a drought, then it is right for everybody based on the universality of moral judgements.
(19) But it would not be right for everybody to do this, based on the generalisation premise.
(20) Therefore, it would not be right for you to do so by *modus tollens*.

Let us state clearly and explicitly the steps in our reasoning by means of which we arrive at this premise:

(i) You are doing or have decided to do a certain thing: watering your lawn during a shortage.
(ii) By arguing with someone who says that what you are doing is wrong, you are defending your action and making a moral claim or judgement, that what you are doing is right.
(iii) Because of the supervenience of moral judgements, you are saying that your action is right by virtue of some of its characteristics, in this case, because it would do more good than harm.
(iv) By virtue of the universality of moral judgements, if claim that it is right for you to act in this way, then you are *ipso facto* saying–whether you like it or not–that it would be okay for anyone and everyone else to do the same thing.

In short, your action and your defence commits you to a moral judgement about your own case; but the universality of moral judgements commits you to applying that same judgement to everyone else. Since you are unwilling to apply it to everyone because you know that it would be bad if everyone did it, you cannot apply it to yourself.

15

The Generalisation Argument and The Basic Teleological Principle

The discussion in Chapter 14 constitutes a good preliminary formulation of the generalisation argument. One of the most important features of this argument is that it fundamentally violates the basic teleological principle–the principle underlying utilitarianism to the effect that one should only do that which will bring about the best consequences; that the right act is the best act. Why is this?

Let us continue using the concrete example of watering the lawn during a drought. I have a large home with ten people living there and a high fence which keeps out anyone I do not want. There is a drought and people have been asked to conserve water. If I conserve water, I will save 100 litres a day. But doing that will not help anyone, since the amount of water this will provide to the other 10 million residents is so minuscule that it cannot even be measured. It will, however, produce a measurable amount of suffering for the ten people living in my house.

If, on the other hand, I do not conserve water, and continue using as much as I want, it will really not hurt anyone. This is because the amount of water other people are going to lack because of my profligacy is not even measurable, and no one else is going to be affected by my behaviour since they will not know about it. It will, however, produce a measurable benefit to the residents in my house; since they will be able to do all those things they could not do if I cut back on my usage.

So, conserving water benefits no one and harms ten people in my household, while continuing to use it as usual, harms no one and benefits ten people. Hence, using water only benefits people without harming anyone, while conserving it only harms people while benefiting absolutely no one. Yet, if the generalisation argument is correct–and we have agreed that it is–using water here would be wrong and conserving it the right thing to do, even though doing so would inflict considerable harm and no good whatsoever.

It is important to note that in a valid application of the generalisation argument, there would be no bad consequences from using the water. It is just that there would be no harm done in the short run. If you can keep it a secret, then there is every reason to believe that your using water in a non-essential way during a drought would harm no one, and there are equally good reasons for thinking that it would, in the long run, have only beneficial consequences. We are also saying that such a course of action would be wrong.

Why? Because of the logical consequences of doing so. By doing so, you are implying that it is the right thing to do. And by claiming that you are right in doing so, you are *ipso facto* claiming that it would also be right if everyone did the same. But you know that it cannot be right for everyone to do so because of the consequences. So by *modus tollens*, if it is not right for everyone, it cannot be right for you.

An Alternative Expression of the Generalisation Argument

Another way of expressing the same argument would be in terms of fairness and undesirable consequences. We can say that there are two different reasons why a given course of action may be rejected as unacceptable. These are if it is either: (a) unfair, or (b) if it involves undesirable consequences. If we have to choose between several alternative courses of action, we could say that any of them with either of these characteristics, i.e. either unfair or undesirable consequences, can be rejected as unacceptable.

From the above example, we can say that there are three possibilities:

(1) No one conserves water.
(2) Everyone conserves water.
(3) Everyone except me and my friends conserve water.

What can we say about each of these examples? Would: (1) be unfair? No, because everyone would be treated the same; everyone is using water as usual. But this alternative would be unacceptable because it would have disastrous consequences. So (1) can be rejected because it would have undesirable consequences although it would be perfectly fair. Possibility (3) would not have undesirable consequences if only my friends and I used water as before, as long as everyone else conserves it. But it would still be unfair; I cannot expect others to make a sacrifice if I am not willing to do the same. Possibility (2) is fair because it treats everyone the same–everyone must conserve water. Neither would it have disastrous consequences. Therefore, we can say, by a process of elimination, that (2) is the only alternative that is neither unfair nor disastrous, and hence the only one that is fair and acceptable.

This can be observed in the table below:

Alternatives	(Un)fairness	Consequences	Result
1. No one conserves	Fair	Disastrous	Unacceptable
2. Everyone conserves	Fair	OK	Acceptable
3. Everyone except me conserves	Unfair	OK	Unacceptable

Conditions for the Valid Application of the Generalisation Argument

What we have discussed so far constitutes the basic structure of the generalisation argument, but it is by no means complete. There are at least two other things that must be considered in order to say whether any specific example is or is not a valid application of the generalisation argument. These are: (i) the epistemological circumstances with respect to how other people will behave, and (ii) the issue of whether or not the behaviour in question involves a benefit or a sacrifice.

Epistemological Circumstances of the Generalisation Argument

There are at least three different epistemological circumstances we can find ourselves in when a generalisation argument is attempted, that is, when someone says, 'You shouldn't do that. What if everyone copied you?' There are three different possibilities with respect to what we may know or believe about what others are doing or are going to do. They are (1) we may know that everyone else or a sufficient number are going to make the sacrifice by conserving water, so that the disaster will be avoided. (2) We may know that no one else or at least an insufficient number is going to make the sacrifice so that the disaster will be inevitable. Or (3) we may not know what someone else is going to do and whether a disaster will be avoided or not.

There are several circumstances that are relevant in determining which of these three possibilities is the case.

(1) *Public awareness.* The matter may be something in which there is general public awareness or none. For example, you may know that if everyone continues to cut down trees for firewood there will eventually be serious consequences–not enough wood for fuel, soil erosion, etc. But you may also know that most other people are totally unaware of this. This would be a genuine different situation, *vis-à-vis* the generalisation argument, than if, you knew that everyone else was aware of the problem.

(2) *Public pronouncements.* One of the ways in which you may know that others are aware of the problem is if there have been public statements about it urging people to conserve firewood; to use more fuel-efficient stoves, etc.

(3) *Appeals by public officials.* Public officials may talk about it and urge people to conserve. The Head of State or a government minister may go on air and say: "We are facing a serious water shortage. I ask everyone to use it only for essential purposes."

(4) *Public directives.* Finally, public officials may not simply urge people to conserve but may or require them to do so through legislation, presidential directives.

Each of these is relevant to the three different epistemological situations in that: (1) If there is no public awareness, then there will be no reason to think that others will make the sacrifice since they would not even be aware of the need for one. Thus, if you know that very few people are aware that the country is facing a scarcity of firewood, then if you ask yourself, 'what are others going to do? Are they going to cut back on the amount of firewood they use?' The answer would have to be 'No.' Since they are not aware of the need for such a sacrifice, there is no way you can expect them to make it. (2) If they are aware of the problem, then there is a possibility that many of them will make the sacrifice. (3) If there has been a public statement urging or even requiring conservation, this certainly constitutes grounds for assuming that others will make the sacrifice.

Now, what bearing do these three epistemological situations have on the validity of any application to the generalisation argument? First, if we know–or have good reasons to believe–that at least a sufficient number of other people are going to make the sacrifice so that the disaster will be averted, then we have an obligation to do likewise. If others are making the sacrifice, you cannot possibly justify your failure to do the same. To do so would clearly be to treat others unfairly; you are asking, expecting and allowing them to do something, which you yourself are not willing to do; and you are benefiting from the fact that they are making the sacrifice. For this, there are no two ways about it.

So let us note that when a sufficient number are making the sacrifice, the generalisation argument applies, meaning that *you are obliged to make the sacrifice.*

How about when no one else is making the sacrifice? We may ask, "Suppose everyone kept on cutting down trees for firewood? There would be no disaster," You might be forced to answer, "Unfortunately, everyone else is doing precisely that and the disaster is already upon us. Not only is there no firewood, but there is also soil erosion, loss of arable land and the result is widespread famine and starvation." So, I may ask: 'Is there any point reason for me not to cut down these few remaining trees?'

This may be a bit cynical, but one response that would not be correct would be 'just because others err and cut down trees for firewood doesn't make it right for you to do it.' This assumes—what is not the case—that what others have done and what you are about to do is, in and of itself, intrinsically wrong.

But this is not so. Cutting down trees for firewood, like watering your lawn, is only wrong in a specific context. It is wrong, for example, where if everyone did so, it would have disastrous consequences. It could also be wrong where there is a prospect that a sufficient number of others are making or will refrain from cutting down trees. In a different context, you might argue that the generalisation argument would not apply: there may be such an abundance of forests that even if everyone cut down trees for firewood, it would not have any bad consequences. Nor would the generalisation argument apply to those countries that have already lost their forests through overuse. Again, there is nothing intrinsically wrong with watering your lawn, or cutting down trees. Such things are wrong only in the context where the generalisation argument validly applies.

(3) The third situation is the most difficult and constitutes one of the most interesting—and difficult—questions in moral philosophy. It revolves around the question of what you are obliged to do when the generalisation question—'suppose everyone did that?'—yields the answer 'It would be a disaster.' Should you stop using water just because if everyone continues using it there will be a disaster – without knowing whether anyone else is going to make this sacrifice? If no one else is going to conserve, your doing so alone will just be a wasted effort, you will suffer for no good reason. If others are making the sacrifice, then I will make it for to do otherwise would be unfair. But if no one else is making the sacrifice then my not doing so would neither be unfair nor would it have undesirable consequences because in such cases, an individual's

actions have no significant consequences. The question here is on what to do if I do not know what others will do?

However, moral common sense would demand that we should make the sacrifice in such a case. This is because, if we say that there is no reason for making the sacrifice, others would be free to argue in the same way, which would be very bad. Unfortunately, this argument is not very satisfactory. We recognise that what we do will have no causal effect on anyone else's actions. We also recognise that what we do will make no difference to what happens for others will make the sacrifice thereby preventing the disaster or they will not thereby causing the disaster.

The generalisation argument only applies to benefits or sacrifices

Our present description of the generalisation argument is still incomplete. Consider the following attempted generalisation argument:

(1) You should not be celibate because if everyone were celibate, it would be a disaster.

This could be elaborated as follows:

(2) If it is okay for you to be celibate, it is okay for everyone.
(3) But it would not be okay for everyone to be celibate.
(4) Therefore, it is not okay for you to be celibate.

Is this a good argument?

A good and sound argument is one which succeeds in proving the truth of its conclusion. Does this argument prove the truth of its conclusion? Is the conclusion true? Is it wrong for you to be celibate because if everyone were so it would be disastrous? Note that if this argument proves that it is wrong for you to be celibate, it would be wrong for anyone else to be so, because this argument would apply to anyone, and not just 'you'.

Certainly, the conclusion that you should not be celibate because of what would happen if everybody were celibate is absurd; the fact that it would be bad if everyone became celibate does not, by itself, prove that no one should be celibate. This is so because we may retort: 'because not everyone is going to be celibate, there is no danger of becoming celibate.' This seems to be a correct response as to why a generalisation argument like (1) is not a good argument and is actually an absurd argument.

Yet note that we have said that the response:

(4) But not everyone is going to water their lawns, cut down trees, etc.,

is not in general a valid rebuttal of the generalisation argument. On the contrary, the fact that others are making the sacrifice is an argument against the application of the generalisation argument. In fact, it is not only an argument against the generalisation argument but it is also one of the conditions that must exist in order for the generalisation argument to apply.

So, the reply in the case of the celibacy example that:

(5) But not everyone is going to be celibate,

is not by itself enough to invalidate this application of the generalisation argument.

Note also that this fallacious application of the generalisation argument could be used against virtually any activity; you want to be a medical doctor–'but what if everyone became a doctor?' Would you want to be a farmer? 'But suppose everyone became a farmer?' That is, whatever example you take, if everyone did the same thing, it would be bad.

So, we could reject the generalisation argument concerning celibacy on the grounds of *reductio ad absurdum:* if this reasoning were correct, no one should do anything. But since this is false, then by *modus tollens,* the argument which leads to it is false.

The problem, however, is that this does not distinguish between the celibacy example, which common sense tells us is a bad argument, and the water shortage example, which common sense tells us is a good argument. Why in one case does it seem relevant to reply 'But not everyone is going to be celibate' while in the other case quite irrelevant to reply 'but not everyone is going to use water non-essentially?'

The answer lies in ascertaining that what is important is not that 'not everyone is going to do that' but rather why they are not. In the case of celibacy, most people are not going to be celibate because they do not want to be celibate. In the case of refraining from using water, if most people are not going to use water in a non-essential way, it is not because they do not want to but because they feel obliged not to– they feel that they ought not to. Not only is it that they do not want to use water, but the opposite is also true. They would like to use water as they normally do. In short, in not using water as usual, they are giving up something, which they see as a benefit and perceive what they are doing as a sacrifice. They would be doing, something they do not like doing and would prefer not to do it.

So, when we say, in the water shortage case, 'suppose everyone did that?' the activity which we are talking about and which the generalisation argument is attempting to show that we should not do is something that is viewed as a benefit. What the argument is trying to show is that what you should do is something that is viewed as a sacrifice. With respect to celibacy, this is not the case. Since not everyone wants to be celibate, being celibate is not something that is generally viewed as beneficial. Thus, not being celibate is not viewed as a sacrifice.

Why does the generalisation argument only seem to apply when we are dealing with things which people want to do and which therefore involve benefits or sacrifices? The generalisation argument essentially involves the notion of fairness or unfairness. When insisting on using water wastefully while expecting that others will not do so, you are treating them unfairly: You are receiving some benefit which you hope others will forego. An individual in such a situation can benefit only if every one else is making a sacrifice. I can benefit by watering my lawn during a drought only if most people are conserving; for if everyone did as I am doing, there would be no water for anyone including myself.

So, when a person insists on violating the conclusion of a valid generalisation argument, he is being unfair. If he insists on watering his lawn even though he realises that if everyone did so there would be no water for anyone, his behaviour would be inherently unfair. He must realise that he can 'get away' with it, only as long as others do not do the same.

What then is the relation between fairness or unfairness and benefit or sacrifice? The issue–the question–of fairness or unfairness only arises in the contexts of benefits or sacrifices.

Fairness or unfairness arises when, for example, I distribute things to others: I can distribute them either fairly or unfairly. However, there will only be a possibility of doing so fairly or unfairly if what I am distributing is something that everyone wants. I will be treating you unfairly if I withhold something from you that I grant to someone else. Yet, you both need it. If only one of you wants it, then by giving it to that person and not to the other, I am not treating the other unfairly because I have not withheld anything from him.

In other words, 'refusing to give you something' really means 'refusing to give you something that you want.' If you do not want it, I cannot, logically, refuse to give it to you, and thus withhold it from you. Similarly, to 'grant you something' really means 'granting you something that you want.' I cannot, logically, grant you something that you do not want. The point is that fairness and unfairness have to do with granting and withholding things, fairly or unfairly.

Take a simple example: I have two books, which all ten students in the class would like to have. As a result, I could distribute them either in a fair or an unfair way. I would do it fairly, for example, if I drew lots; and unfairly, if I gave them to the two most attractive female students, with the hope of getting something in return. But if no one wanted these books, then it would be impossible for me to give them away unfairly or fairly. This is because the books would not be things, which anyone wanted. Thus acquiring them would neither be considered a benefit nor would failing to get them be considered a loss.

We can therefore note why the generalisation argument only applies where benefits or sacrifices are involved. A 'benefit' is something that is wanted and its absence or loss is a sacrifice. Hence, if whatever is involved in a purported generalisation argument is not something that is viewed as a benefit or sacrifice, then it will not be something that people want. As a result, the very possibility of fairness or unfairness, will not arise. If there is no question of fairness or unfairness then there will be no question of applying the generalisation argument, since the generalisation argument involves one person treating others unfairly.

Reformulation of the Generalisation Argument

In light of the above, we can now explain why the celibacy example was not a valid application of the generalisation argument, 'What if everyone was celibate?' The answer is that it would be very bad. That, however, is irrelevant because in this case not everyone is going to be celibate. More important, the reason why they are not going to be celibate is that they have no wish to be.

Instead of asking:

(6) Suppose everyone was celibate?

We should ask:

(7) Suppose everyone who wishes was celibate?

The answer to this question would not mean much. Given that most people do not want to be celibate even if all the people who wish were celibate, they would not be very many. As a result, it would not have much effect, and certainly it would not lead to the extinction of the human race as it would if everyone were celibate.

Reformulated version of the celibacy example

Let us reformulate the above example of the generalisation argument as follows:

(8) If it is right for one to be celibate because he wants to be, it would be alright for everyone who wishes to be celibate.
(9) It would not be okay for everyone who wishes to be celibate.
(10) Therefore, it is not okay for one to be celibate.

Is this a good argument? Does it establish its conclusion as true? Even if we assume that it is still valid–such that if the premises were true, the conclusion would also have to be true–it will only prove its conclusion if both of its premises are true. But are they?

We can assume that the first premise is true: if it is okay for one to be celibate because he wants to be, then it would be okay for anyone else. But how about the second premise–that it would not be right for everyone who wishes to be celibate? Since not many people would want to be celibate, then even if all people who did want to be celibate were, it would have no significant consequences; it would not matter if, say 1 or 2% of the population were celibate. Hence, the second premise of this reformulated generalisation argument is not true. Therefore, the argument does not prove that its conclusion–that one ought not to be celibate–is true. This is precisely the result we want, because the conclusion is not true.

Thus, this reformulated version of the generalisation argument does not fall victim to the problem which plagued the original formulation, i.e., that of leading to a false conclusion. The original formulation [(2)–(4)] had something wrong with it; for if its argument were correct, it would have meant that it would be wrong for anyone to be celibate. Since that conclusion is absurd, we infer, by *modus tollens*, that there is something wrong with the original formulation of the argument.

The reformulated version of the generalisation argument does not suffer from this defect because in it, the argument does not prove that it would be wrong to be celibate; it does not prove this because its second premise is false.

We note, however, that the water shortage example remains under this reformulation version, thus:

(11) If it is okay for one to use water because he wants to, then it is okay for anyone else who wants to.
(12) But it would not be okay for everyone who wants to use the water.
(13) Therefore, it is not okay for him to use water in non-essential way.

In this case, the second premise remains true because most people would want to use water as they usually do (unlike the case of celibacy), then if we ask our generalisation question:

Suppose everyone wants to use water in a wasteful manner?

The answer would be:

It would be very bad.

In other words, the reformulated generalisation premise:

If everyone wanted to use water in a wasteful way it would be very bad,

would be true.

Hence, this argument would remain a valid application of the generalisation argument, since we have accepted it as a philosophical datum that it is a good argument.

Celibacy and the Generalisation Argument

Note that there are circumstances in which the celibacy example would be a valid application of the generalisation argument. Given our analysis so far, it should not be difficult to see what these circumstances would be. In general, they would have to be circumstances in which the answer to the reformulated generalisation question:

What if everyone who wanted to be was celibate?

would be the reformulated generalisation premise, that is, circumstances in which it was true is that:

If everyone who wanted to be were celibate, it would be very bad.

And that would be the case if, for some reason, most people wanted to be celibate or at least childless. For if most people wanted to be celibate and actually became celibate then it would mean the end of the human race.

So all we need to do to find the circumstances in which the celibacy example would be a valid application of the generalisation argument is to imagine circumstances in which most people would want to be celibate. Assume there is a nuclear holocaust, leaving only a few thousand survivors from whom reproduction become extremely difficult. Under such circumstances having children might be a great burden, which individuals would want to avoid at all costs since it would be difficult to fend even for oneself.

In such a situation, it might well be true that:

> If everyone who wishes remained celibate, it would be a disaster.

In such a situation, not being celibate would be a sacrifice and being celibate a benefit. In such a situation it would be wrong to be celibate and the generalisation argument would apply. Under these circumstances, the second premise (9) of the reformulated version of the generalisation argument would be true, and so the argument [(8) -(10)] would be a sound argument which would prove the conclusion that it would be wrong, under such circumstances, to remain celibate.

'Exceptions' to the Generalisation Argument

It is important to note that the valid application of the generalisation argument rarely, if ever, requires that everyone make the sacrifice–at least not in order to avoid the disastrous consequences. It is enough that a sufficient number of people make it.

Thus, it is not necessary, in order to prevent a disaster, that everyone conserves water; it is enough if a certain percentage does it. It would not be necessary, that everyone should volunteer for military service in time of war; there is a certain percentage that would be sufficient, and beyond that number would not only be unnecessary, it might even be undesirable. How do we decide who would be exempted from military service?

A necessary condition for any group to be exempted is that the group's exemption can be generalised. That is, if we ask the question:

> Suppose everyone in the group was exempted?

Here, a further question would ensue, namely: Would it be a disaster or would it be alright? If the answer is that there would be a disaster if not enough people were called up to defend the country, then the exemption cannot be generalised. If the answer was that it would be alright, then the exemption would at least be a possible.

The Generalisation Argument and the Basic Teleological Principle

Let us assume it is suggested that everyone between the ages of 18-45 years must serve in the military. How would we decide what the age limits should be? Presumably, very young children, as well as the very old and infirm men are not fit for service. But why 45 instead of 40 or 35 or 50? And why 18 instead of 15 or 20? In other words, what is the justification for saying that 'everyone below 18 or above 35 needs not serve?' Or that 'everyone except those below 18 or over 35 must serve?' To answer this question, we must come up with statements, which can be generalised. We must ask: 'suppose everyone below 18 and above 35 were exempted, would that have disastrous consequences? The answer to this question is entirely a matter of empirical and contingent fact, depending on: (i) how large the population is, which you have to draw from, and (ii) how many people you actually need.

If you are a small country like Israel but need a large army, and then ask whether if everyone below 18 and above 35 is exempted it would it be bad? The answer would be, 'Yes.' Since Israel only has a population of about 8 million and needs an army of 800,000. If it recruited only men aged between 18 and 35, it would only get 400,000. Therefore, it must take everyone between 18 and 50.

Moreover, while most countries exempt women from military service, Israel does not. Presumably, the reason is that its population and security needs are such that if asked: 'What if all females and those men below 18 and above 50 were exempted?' The answer would be that there wouldn't be enough to fulfil the military requirements. Hence, women cannot be exempted.

In a country the size of the United State of America with a population of well over 280 million and requiring a military establishment not much bigger than Israel's, it can afford to exempt females and only take males between 18 and 26 to serve. This is because the generalisation 'only males between 18 and 26 are required for military service' does not lead to disastrous consequences. Even within that group, there are all kinds of exemptions: married men, university students, employees in essential industries, men from families that have lost men in previous wars. They have all, at various times, been exempted.

However, in Israel there are very few exemptions. Nearly everyone must serve.

Why are all these exemptions allowed in the United States and not in Israel? The answer: The number from which the military selects in the United States is so large in comparison to its needs that, even if you allow all the people in the categories mentioned, there will still be more than enough remaining. In Israel, on the other hand, if you were to exempt only men from families who had lost someone in a previous war, you certainly would not have enough.

One group that is exempted in Israel are the very orthodox religious people; they are not required to undergo military service. Why not? One necessary condition for allowing this exemption is that the number of such people is so small that even if all of them were exempted it would not have bad consequences–there would still be enough people to fulfil the military needs. In other words, it would not make any difference. But if it was the case that the number of orthodox religious people was sufficiently large and all of them were to be exempted, it would have very bad consequences, then they would not be exempted.

Examples of the Generalisation Argument

Let us briefly consider two other examples of the generalisation argument, concerning voting and queuing:

The obligation to vote

Most of us would agree that if we live in a democracy where we have the right to vote, then we have an obligation to vote–and that it is wrong to neglect this obligation. But it is not easy to say exactly why this should be so.

Assume I am on my way to vote, and bump into you going in the opposite direction. 'Aren't you voting?' I ask. 'No, I am too busy,' you answer. Suppose everyone acted like you and did not vote because it was not convenient? It would be very bad because there would be no election and eventually no democracy.

You might then answer. 'Certainly, my vote is: (i) not going to make any difference and; (b) since no one knows that I am not voting, it cannot cause anyone else not to vote.' Stated differently, the outcome of the election will be the same with or without my one vote. If my candidate is going to lose, by say 10,000 votes without my vote, then even with it he would still have lost, though by 9,999 votes instead of 10,000; but that makes no difference at all–the result will still be the same. If, on the other hand, he was going to win without my vote by 10,000, then even with my vote, he would just win by 10,001–which does not make much difference.

What this means is that, if he is going to lose, by anything more than one vote, my voting will not do him any good; and if he is going to win even by just one vote, he does not need my vote. The only condition in which my vote would make a difference would be in the highly unlikely possibility that without my vote, the two candidates would get exactly the same number of votes. Therefore, with my vote, my candidate would win by one vote.

Though the possibility that with my vote my man would win by one vote is extremely remote, it is practically speaking impossible. This is because in any closely contested election, there is always a recount. And one thing that is virtually certain is that when you have a recount, the result always differs from the original by at least several votes, which means that my one vote would not have made any difference even in the case of such an election.

In short, if you are going to try to convince this person that he ought to vote because every vote counts and that his vote will make a difference, you will have difficult times. The probability that his one vote will actually make a difference to the outcome of the election is so remote that it can, for all practical purposes, be ignored.

Yet it is somehow true that every vote counts. If that wasn't the case, then there would be no democracy. And the aggregate of many people voting is made up of each and every individual. So each vote does count.

Despite this, everything that has been said in rebuttal of our original statement that one ought to vote is true. The chances that one vote can make a difference to the outcome of an election is almost nil, and the outcome would be the same with or without this one vote.[3] "Moreover, since my voting is a private affair, it will not affect anyone else's behaviour." Yet, we know that it would be wrong not to vote just because it is inconvenient; we know that everyone living in a democratic society has an obligation to vote. We can also note that the generalisation argument as expressed by the question 'suppose everyone did that?' is a good argument. By now we should, however, be able to say why and how it is.

We are not, when we ask 'suppose everyone did that?' saying that because you do this others will; we recognise that what you do will have no effect on what others do. We may also know that regardless of what you do, most other people are going to vote. There may well be a strong tradition of high voter turnouts.

None of that makes any difference to the generalisation argument. The argument is not that if you do not then, others will not. That if you claim to be justified in not voting because it is inconvenient, then everyone else would be equally justified in not voting because it is inconvenient. Since, we have already agreed that it would be a disaster if everyone failed to vote, by *modus tollens*, you are therefore, not justified in not voting because it is inconvenient. In other words:

> (14) If it were alright for you not to vote because it is inconvenient, it would be alright for everyone not to vote due to the same reason.
> (15) But it would not be alright for everyone not to vote.
> (16) Therefore, it is improper for you not to vote.

Note that the condition of involving a benefit or a sacrifice is satisfied. With fairness, voting for most people is an inconvenience and would therefore confer a benefit of not taking the trouble to vote. Most people take the trouble because they realise, perhaps

---

[3] Despite the improbability of a tie in general elections and hence the slim chance that only one vote may determine the outcome, this is not to say that it is impossible. Indeed, during the December 2007 general elections in Kenya, there a tie in Dujis constituency in North Eastern province.

without thinking about it, that they have some sort of obligation to vote. Thus, although the sacrifice is very small, and the benefit one would get by neglecting to vote equally slight, it is still viewed as a benefit or sacrifice. If you could imagine circumstances in which it would not be viewed as any kind of sacrifice–but where most people positively enjoyed voting–then we do not think the generalisation argument would apply.

Queuing

Nearly, everyone recognises that it is wrong to jump a queue including those who do so. But few would be able to give a good argument showing why it is wrong. Most people would say that it is wrong because one makes others wait longer. But the amount of time one might cause others to wait may be negligible; instead of waiting 10 minutes, they may have to wait 10 minutes and 15 seconds. One may save himself or herself half an hour of waiting, which could certainly outweigh the tiny loss that everyone else will suffer.

There is of course a difference between this and the voting example. Here, your action is by its nature open and public. Others in the queue may notice you and this may cause some of them to jump the queue. If it does, then you would have a more or less straightforward utilitarian argument for not jumping the queue just because someone else has done so. So, you may then jump the queue with impunity.

But the argument is: 'If you claim that it is okay for you to jump the queue, then you are *ipso facto* claiming that it would be okay for anyone else and everybody to do so.' If everyone jumped the queue, there would be a queue no more just a mob pushing and shoving and everyone would suffer. Nevertheless, if you were correct in saying that it would be alright for you to jump the queue, you would in effect be saying that it would be alright for everyone else to do the same. But since you agree that it would not be alright for everyone to do it then you cannot claim that it is alright for you to do the same. Thus:

> (17) If it is okay for you to jump the queue, it would be okay if everyone did so.

(18) But it would not be okay if everyone jumped the queue.

(19) Therefore, it is not okay for you to jump the queue.

Note that the benefit or sacrifice conditions are satisfied here. Even in a very law-abiding society, where people patiently wait in queues, they would prefer not to have to queue; they would prefer if they could get served immediately rather than having to wait for some time. So, waiting in this case is a sacrifice.

16

Rule-Utilitarianism

Rule-Utilitarianism is offered as an alternative to utilitarianism and deontology. Rule-utilitarianism is basically an attempt to apply the generalisation argument to actions, which are not, in and of themselves, intrinsically wrong. Watering your lawn, cutting down trees, etc., are not intrinsically wrong. They are only wrong in a certain context, i.e., where in case everyone did them, it would be very bad.

Rule-utilitarianism, in effect, applies similar reasoning to things that are intrinsically wrong – breaking a promise, lying, and punishing an innocent man. These are things which the deontologist would give no argument as to why they are wrong, but would just say: 'They are wrong because they are wrong.' Rule-utilitarianism attempts to provide an argument to explain why these things–which are not wrong in certain contexts but are *prima facie* wrong anywhere and at all times–are wrong.

The Rule-Utilitarian Theory of Punishment

This is a very contentious area of dispute between act-utilitarianism (utilitarianism) and deontology. The act-utilitarian says that the principle of utility can and should be applied to each and every individual action. For example, I can argue that I am justified in punishing someone if doing so will bring about the best results. The deontologist, on the other hand, would say that on the basis of that criterion, one would be justified in doing things that our moral common sense would tell us are wrong.

So if all that mattered were the beneficial results of punishment, the deontologist would not agree; for we could fake punishment so that potential criminals are deterred and thus achieving this beneficial result of punishment; while at the same time letting the criminal go free and thus preventing pain and suffering by the criminal and his family. To the utilitarian, this would obviously be much better than actually punishing the criminal, and would therefore be what we actually ought to do. However, the deontologist would argue that our moral common sense tells us that this would not be the right thing to do.

At face value, the deontologist appears to be right: act-utilitarianism seems to sanction such actions and we would certainly not say are right. But when you ask the deontologist why it is wrong to let a guilty person go free or even worse, to punish an innocent person, he would not give a logically satisfactory answer. He can only give an answer such as: *'it is self-evidently wrong, it is in and of itself wrong and there is nothing more that can be said about it.'*

It is here that the rule-utilitarian claims to be able to provide an argument to prove that these things are wrong, without having to appeal to 'intuition.' The rule-utilitarian claims that there is a better way to avoid the conclusion that it would be alright to let the guilty person go free other than appealing to such 'ultimate' moral facts. He of course agrees that it would be wrong to let a guilty person go free, but he would want to prove this without having to say 'it is wrong because it is wrong.'

Suppose we asked: 'What if everyone allowed a guilty person to go free, would that do more good than actually punishing him?' We are not saying that everyone else is going to do that, because we recognise that the whole point of such an act would be to keep it secret. Instead, we are saying that, on the basis of the universality of moral judgements, if you, the person in authority, are justified in letting a guilty person go free because you think that will be good, it would follow that anyone else with similar authority will be justified in acting that way. In other words, it would *ipso facto* follow that anyone in such a position would be equally justified in doing the same thing.

Expressed differently—and this is one of the most important points here—when you say that it would be alright for you to let a guilty person free this cannot apply only to you. You are *ipso facto* endorsing a certain general practice or legal system whereby anyone in authority is entitled to let a guilty person go free if he thinks that it will do the most good. That is because you cannot say that it would be alright for you to do this without, at the same time, saying that it would be alright for anyone in a similar position to do the same.

This means that one cannot consider just his own case. You must bear in mind the rule or law that would allow you and anyone else in a similar position to do this. That is because, by virtue of the universality of moral judgements, in claiming that it is alright for you to do something you are *ipso facto* saying that it would be alright for anyone and everyone else to do it.

So, the rule-utilitarian says that in determining such a case what we have to consider is a certain legal system. And this legal system would amount to giving anyone in authority—police, chiefs, magistrates, etc.—the right to decide whether or not to punish individuals on the basis of act-utilitarianism. That is, on the basis of whether or not, it would be appropriate to punish the person or let him go free.

When we realise that this is what we must consider—having such a legal system and not deciding in just this one case—we can see that it would be a good thing. On the contrary, a legal system which allowed individuals to make such decisions would be a disaster. This would be so because, it would be subject to all kinds of abuse; friends of guilty persons would pay to get them freed; enemies of innocent people would do the same to get them punished. More importantly, people would not know when someone is 'punished' whether he was really guilty or was being 'punished', for the public good; potential criminals might think that if they are caught they might be freed instead of being punished. It is likely therefore, that such a legal system would fail to serve the major utilitarian goal of deterrence and would lead to a general state of uncertainty, disorder, and anarchy.

Note that our rejection of such a legal system–and hence of the individual case that entails it–does not appeal to deontological principles. Such a legal system would be wrong not because it would be unjust to put innocent people in prison, but because it would lead to chaos and disorder. Fundamentally also, if we reject such a legal system, then we cannot justify the individual case whose defence entails the system.

Legal System Based on Act-Utilitarian Principles

A legal system based on act-utilitarian principles would not only be disastrous but also incoherent–that is, it would involve a kind of self-contradiction.

What, specifically, would such a legal system be like? It would have to contain something of this order:

> (20) When sheriff or a police chief believes that he can stage a fake punishment in such a way that the public will falsely believe that the guilty person has been punished, thereby achieving the utilitarian goal of deterring other potential criminals, then he is authorised to set the guilty person free provided he is certain that the person will commit no further crimes. He will thereby achieve the other utilitarian goal of preventing the suffering of the criminal and his family.

Now one essential feature of this law would be that it requires public officials to deceive the public since by faking the punishment, the aim is to make the public believe that the person has been punished when in reality he has not. So, it involves deception. [Note, however, that we are not saying that the system is intrinsically wrong, for that would be to appeal to deontological principles, which we cannot do. Our aim is to prove by appealing only to utilitarian considerations–plus the uniformity of moral judgements–that such a system cannot be justified].

A second important feature of this or any law is that, by its very nature, it must be publicly known. The idea of having laws–for example, prohibiting anyone under 18 from driving a motor vehicle–but keep these laws secret, is absurd, for the purpose of having laws is to regulate people's conduct. It would certainly be impossible to regulate people's conduct if the people whose conduct you wish to regulate do not know about the laws. We can therefore say that one essential feature of any law is that it must be publicly stated.

Now let us consider this law (20). The law is saying that when people are found guilty of a crime, the authorities will tell the public that they are being punished, so that they will be deterred from committing similar crimes but will actually not punish them. But if this law were to be publicly stated, then it would amount to asserting the following:

> (21) We hereby announce to the general public that when someone is found guilty of a crime, we will tell you that they are being punished to act as a deterrent, though in fact they will actually not be punished but will instead be set free.

This would be absurd. It would amount to asking me the time and I tell you it is 5 o'clock but for some reason, I want to deceive you into thinking it is 6 o'clock, and so I tell you:

> (22) I am going to deceive you: I am going to tell you that it is 6 o'clock while in fact it is 5 o'clock.

Normally, if one person wants to deceive another, he must keep the fact of his deception secret from the person he wishes to deceive. He can tell others that he is deceiving you, but he cannot reveal to you.

In the Dreyfus Affair if the utilitarians had tried to state their view publicly as opposed to keeping it amongst themselves, they would have had to say:

> (23) Dreyfus is innocent but in order to avoid the public turmoil that may result from admitting his innocence and freeing him, we are going to keep him in prison and tell the public that he is guilty.

Just as this would be absurd and self-contradictory, it can be debated whether the legal system would be justified either in freeing this guilty person or punishing the innocent person reasoning out that it would do more good than harm.

It might be thought, however, that such a law need not be known to the public in its entirety, but only to those officials dealing with the prescribed punishment. The reason allowing for the fake punishment and release could be kept secret instead of being written as part of the public law. But even if that was theoretically possible, practically speaking, it is not. Law must be written down somewhere or be based on legal precedent. The latter is by its nature public, while the statutory or written law, even if it was in the statue books or hidden from the public, would in a democratic and open society, just be impractical and unworkable. Eventually, such a law would become publicly known with disastrous consequences. [It is worth noting that the Catholic Church reportedly tried for centuries to keep the Bible away from the 'common people' for fear that they would 'misinterpret' it. This didn't work and apparently had disastrous consequences].

The rule-utilitarian has, by using the generalisation argument, proved and explained why it would be wrong to let a guilty person go free reasoning it would do more good than harm. One would do this without having to appeal to deontological considerations of intrinsic right or wrong and moral intuitions.

For example,

(24) If it is okay for you to let this guilty person go free because it will do the most good, it would be okay to have a legal system in which all guilty persons would go free if it would do the most good.

(25) But it would not be okay to have such a legal system.

(26) Therefore, it would not be okay for you to let these guilty persons go free because it will do the most good.

If this argument applies to you, it will equally apply to anyone, so that it would be wrong for anyone to let a guilty person go free just because it would do the most good.

Using the generalisation argument, we can show that a legal system in which individual decisions about punishment are made on the basis of act-utilitarian principles would have disastrous consequences.

So, a legal system that is based solely on what is the best thing to do in each and every individual case would be a disaster and hence can be rejected on utilitarian grounds.

The rule-utilitarian further says that deciding individual cases on grounds of utility would be very bad. The legal system that would in fact be the best and that may be the only system that is workable, is one in which people are punished if they are guilty. This amounts to saying that the best legal system, in terms of utilitarian considerations–indeed the only workable one–is a system in which individual cases are decided on deontological grounds. Having laws which say in effect:

> If a person is found guilty of a crime he should be punished, not because that it is the best thing to do, but because he is guilty of an offence or rather 'because he deserves to be punished.'

According to the rule-utilitarian, having such laws will in the long run, have the best consequences. A society in which people are punished only when they are guilty will be a much better society–on strictly utilitarian grounds–than one in which people are punished when in each individual case, it will do the most good.

Hence, the rule-utilitarian argues that we can justify our moral common sense judgements that a person should be punished if he is guilty even if more good could be done by letting him go free. And similarly, that a person should not be punished if he is innocent even if punishing him would do more good. In both cases, he is arguing without appealing to deontological 'intuitions'. It is wrong to punish an innocent person because to think otherwise–on the grounds of utility–is automatically to endorse a certain kind of legal system in which individual cases of punishment are always decided on the grounds of utility. But such a legal system, if seen in detail, would be totally unacceptable on strictly utilitarian grounds. And since you would not want to endorse such a legal system in which this is done, you cannot endorse doing so in one case since to endorse the latter is to automatically endorse the former.

Rule-Utilitarianism and Promising

Let us now apply rule-utilitarianism to the obligation to keep promises. The act-utilitarian says that the utilitarian principle can and should be applied to each and every individual case of promising; we should keep a promise only if doing so will do the most good. The deontologist says that this is absurd because if you make a promise, you have a *prima facie* obligation to keep it independent of the consequences. This is because it is intrinsically right to keep a promise and intrinsically wrong to break it. It is an 'ultimate' moral fact and there is no answer to the question why one has some obligation; it is just a self-evident fact that he does. But the rule-utilitarian claims to have an argument to explain why we have such an obligation, which does not depend on any appeal to 'ultimate' moral acts and 'intuitions'.

This argument amounts to applying the generalisation argument to promising and asking the question: What if everyone broke a promise because they thought it was the best thing to do?

Thus:

(27) If it is alright for you to break your promise just because you think that it is the best thing to do, then it would be alright for anyone else to do so. In other words, to endorse breaking a promise for some reason is automatically to endorse an institution–practice–which everyone would subscribe to.

(28) But it would not be alright for everyone to behave this way, that is, such a generally accepted practice would not be acceptable on utilitarian grounds.

(29) Therefore, it would not be alright for you to break your promise just because you thought it was the best thing to do.

In other words, to have, as an accepted practice, that people only keep promises when they think that it will do the others most good would mean that there would be nothing like promising. However, that would, at best, be a disaster and, at worst, render civilised society impossible. That in effect is what a person is advocating when he says that he is justified in breaking a promise because *it will do the most good*. Again, on the basis of the universality of moral judgements, if you claim it is alright for you to do something, you are automatically saying that it is alright for anyone else to do so. Thus, the rule-utilitarian is saying that an institution or moral rule in which everyone was free to decide whether or not to keep each individual promise on the basis of utilitarian considerations, can be rejected on utilitarian grounds.

The only alternative to such a useless 'system' is one in which every person, when making a promise, undertakes–and understands himself as undertaking–a *prima facie* obligation to do what he has promised to do, irrespective of any consequences. Such a system–institution or practice–would be the best system in terms of utility, for it would mean that people would be able to rely on others, trust them to tell the truth, to do what they say they will do, etc. A system in which people act in their own individual ways as if they were deontologists, that is: *'I have made a promise, therefore I must keep it barring, extreme consequences'*, can be justified on utilitarian grounds. For a system in which everyone thought and acted as if they were deontologists, accepting a *prima facie* obligation to keep promises regardless of any consideration of the consequences, would benefit society as a whole and be in everyone's interest. A society where such a system is universally practised would be far better than a society in which such a system is absent, for example, one in which an act-utilitarian system was practised.

Rule-Utilitarianism and the obligation to be truthful

What has been said above also applies to our obligation to be truthful. A society in which people's word can be relied on is a much better society–on strictly utilitarian grounds–than one in which that is not the case. Which is a better place to live in–one in which everyone is distrustful and suspicious of others or one in which everyone trusts others and can rely on another's word? Obviously, the latter. But to justify lying just because it is the best thing to do in that particular case is to advocate for a society in which everyone would be a liar; it is to advocate for a society in which people cannot trust one another.

Rule-Utilitarianism and stealing

Imagine living in a society where everyone is afraid of being attacked and robbed, having to put all kinds of locks on doors, line guards, being afraid to go out of their houses at night and so on. On the other hand, imagine living in a society where one is safe all the time and does not have to worry about thieves breaking into his house in the middle of the night. Which of the two is a better society to live in?

Certainly the latter. The point is that the rule-utilitarian says that it is wrong to steal without resorting to saying 'it is wrong because it is wrong.' Rather, he says that for a person to claim that it is not wrong to steal endorses a society in which everyone lives in fear. And since he cannot endorse that kind of society, he cannot claim that it is alright to take something that is not his.

A society in which people are honest–think and behave as deontologists–is the society that dishonest people can flourish. This is precisely because everyone trusts the other hence making it very easy for a dishonest person to lie, cheat and steal. So he would benefit as a result of others' willingness to make sacrifices which he himself is not willing to make.

Rule-utilitarianism – A Summary

Rule-utilitarianism consists of applying the generalisation argument to all questions of morality. It applies to things such as watering ones lawn during a drought, jumping a queue, which are not viewed as being intrinsically wrong and whose only basis is something like the generalisation argument. It also applies to things which we think are intrinsically wrong, for example, breaking a promise, stealing and punishing the innocent, etc. It therefore attempts to give a general explanation or theory of all our common sense moral judgements.

Rule-utilitarianism asserts that practises such as promising, telling the truth and punishment can be justified on utilitarian grounds; their general acceptance will have beneficial consequences and their non-existence will have disastrous consequences. These institutions or generally accepted rules or practices rest on the fact that individuals are not free to decide individual cases on utilitarian grounds. Such rules stipulate that individual acts must be decided on the basis of certain deontological rules. The rule-utilitarian asserts that everyone will be better off, on utilitarian grounds, if everyone acts and thinks like the deontologist, that is, does not make decisions in individual cases on the basis of utility, but makes them on the basis of deontological rules.

It is worth noting that the rule-utilitarian is not really disagreeing with the deontologist's point of view. He simply goes beyond it. He would say to the deontologist:

> You are right in saying that if we have made a promise we have a *prima facie* obligation to keep it irrespective of any other consideration; that, if a person is innocent, he must not be punished for the simple reason that he is innocent independent of the consequences. You may say, if you want, that it is 'intrinsically wrong' to break a promise or imprison an innocent person, and I would even agree that this is what we should believe. But whereas you can give no explanation for why we should believe that, I can. We should believe such things because
>
> believing them is socially useful. A society in which everyone believes in them and acts upon them will be a much better society than one in which people do not believe in them. Or even better: that civilised society would not be possible unless such things were generally believed.

Note that while the rule-utilitarian is saying that if you ask:

> What would happen if everyone broke promises whenever it was convenient to do so?

The answer would be that *it would be a disaster*. In other words, such a proposition cannot be generalised. But if you ask: on the other hand:

> (30) What would happen if everyone broke a promise when the consequences of keeping it would be extremely bad, for example, someone might be in danger of losing his life as in the example of having to break a promise in order to take an injured person to the hospital?

The answer would presumably be that no bad consequences would result since this kind of situation cannot happen very frequently. Therefore, the number of such cases is sufficiently small such that even if everyone in such an extreme situation broke their promise, it would not have any undesirable consequences.

Hence, (30) would not constitute a valid application of the generalisation argument and thus the rule-utilitarian theory of promising would not contradict our moral common sense on this point. For it is part of our moral common sense that in such situations, we are justified in breaking promises. The conclusion of rule-utilitarian with respect to promising would be that we have a *prima facie* obligation to keep promises but this can be outweighed by other utilitarian considerations.

In general, the rule-utilitarian's conclusion about our obligation will coincide with the deontologist's since what the rule-utilitarian is saying is that we should all think like deontologists. The only difference is that he claims to have a theory or explanation as to why we should think like the deontologist other than saying that it is a matter of 'intuition' about 'ultimate moral facts.' We should think like deontologists, the rule-utilitarian says, because a society in which everyone thinks like a deontologist will be the best society–on utilitarian grounds. Or that no society can function or exist unless most people act and think like deontologists.

Review Exercises

1. Consider the statement:

   Abortion is considered wrong in Kenya, but in other places, e.g, in Japan, it is accepted as being right.

   Assume that this statement is true. Explain clearly whether or not it supports ethical relativism.

2. Explain clearly the difference between the following two statements:

   (i) *In some parts of Kenya, cannibalism is not considered wrong.*

   (ii) *Cannibalism is not wrong.*

3. Consider the following statement:

   Moral standards differ from one time or place to another.

   (a) Is this statement true?

   (b) If it is true, explain why it does or does not support ethical relativism.

4. Using your own examples, explain the difference between cultural or belief relativism and ethical relativism.

5. (a) What is the difference between unrestricted ethical relativism and restricted ethical relativism?

   (b) What are the two possible versions of restricted ethical relativism?

   (c) How can restricted ethical relativism be shown to involve a contradiction? Relate this to the two principles of belief.

6. "Every society known to man has an incest taboo." Would this statement, if true, be evidence for ethical relativism, ethical absolutism, or neither of the two? Explain.

7. Consider the following conversation:

   Brian: *Human pain and suffering is always bad.*

   Randie: *Having a tooth drilled by a dentist is painful, but if it saves your tooth; it is not bad.*

   Explain exactly why Randie's reply is or is not correct?

8. Assume that the following statement is true:

   Tartness makes any mango good.

   Does it follow from this that every tart mango is good? Explain clearly why or why not.

9. (a) Describe fully the circumstances under which the following two statements would both be true:

   (i) *Polygamy in Central province is wrong.*

   (ii) *Polygamy in Western province is not wrong.*

   (b) Explain and state clearly what each of them would imply if they are both to be true.

   (c) Explain exactly why if they are understood in this way, they do or do not constitute any evidence for ethical relativism.

10. Consider the following discussion:

    Brian: *This is a good mango.*

    Randie: *I disagree, I don't think it is.*

    What are the two different types of disagreement that this discussion could be expressing? Describe specifically the circumstances under which it is likely to be expressing one or the other.

11. Consider the statement:

    It is always wrong to violate moral customs.

    How could this statement be understood so that it is considered plausible? Would it, if true, offer any support to ethical relativism? Explain why or why not.

12. Consider the statement:

    All mangoes in this box are good.

    What are the different ways in which this statement might be understood, and do any of these ways constitute moral judgements?

13. Explain clearly how the following two statements can both be true, and describe the circumstances under which it would be so.

    (i) *Cannibalism is wrong.*

    (ii) *There are times when cannibalism may not be wrong.*

14. Explain how the following statements can both be true.

    (i) *Other things being equal, the smaller a computer is, the better.*

    (ii) *Other things being equal, the larger a computer is, the better.*

    [NB: The answer to this question involves the difference between good-making characteristics and good-indicating characteristics].

15. Can 'being traditional' be a good-making characteristic?

    Or

    Can it be a good-indicating characteristic? Explain.

16. What is meant by a 'hybrid' judgment?

    Using examples explain whether such judgements are moral judgements or not.

17. (a) What is the basic teleological principle?

    (b) Explain how the basic teleological principle can seem self-evident when in fact it is probably not true.

18. What is meant by the 'subjectivity' problem? Is it a problem peculiar to utilitarianism? Explain.

19. What is the difference between *the objectively right act* and *the subjectively right act*? Which one ought we engage in? Explain.

20. Using examples, explain what saying that "utilitarianism is future-looking while deontology is past-looking", means.

21. Using examples, explain the difference between saying that "something is wrong independent of the consequences" and saying that "it is wrong no matter what the consequences."

22. Does the deontologist say that we have an obligation to keep promises *no matter what the consequences* or merely that we have an obligation *independent of the consequences?* Explain using examples.

23. State clearly the argument, which the deontologist uses against the utilitarian concerning deathbed promises. How does this argument involve *modus tollens*?

24. What are the basic strengths and weaknesses of the utilitarian theory of punishment versus the strengths and weaknesses of the deontological theory of punishment?

25. How does the concept of justice differ from that of right or wrong in terms of the difference between *'wrong independent of the consequences'* and *'wrong no matter what the consequences?'*

26. Exactly what does it mean to say that *moral judgements concerning justice are absolute?*

27. How do questions of justice illustrate the notion of formalism?

28. Using examples, illustrate the difference between *a moral theory* and *a moral view*.

29. Using examples, explain the difference between the following moral views (not theories) of punishment:

    (i) a utilitarian view
    (ii) a restricted retributivist view
    (iii) an unrestricted retributivist view

    Which of the views is, in effect, a formalist view?

30. Is *formalism* a moral view or a moral theory? Explain.

31. Are *utilitarianism* and *deontology* moral views or moral theories? Explain.

32. Was the position taken by the officers who said that Dreyfus should not be released *a moral view* or *a moral theory*? Explain.

33. What is the relevance of the Dreyfus affair with respect to the theoretical dispute between the utilitarian and the deontologist? What is the argument against the position of the utilitarian, with respect *to secrecy* versus *public disclosure*?

34. (a) How can it be argued that in the utilitarian theory, there is no such thing as promising?

    (b) Exactly how does this conclusion constitute an argument against utilitarianism?

35. What exactly is the relation between the deontological theory of punishment and the issue of recidivism?

36. What is the connection between *promising* and the existence of language? How can this be used as an argument against utilitarianism?

37. What is the difference between *how much* a person is punished and *how* he is punished? How is this distinction important with respect to the deontologist's attitude toward such things as recidivism?

38. Consider the statement:

    The deontologist-retributivist is not concerned at all with the deterrent effect of punishment.

    Is it true or false? Explain.

Bibliography

Abelson, R. *Ethics for Modern Life.* New York: St. Martins Press, 1995.

Acton, H.B. (ed.) *The Philosophy of Punishment.* London: MacMillan, 1969.

Albert, E.M. *Great Traditions in Ethics.* Belmont: Wadsworth Publishing Co., 1984.

Allen, C.K. *Aspects of Justice.* London: Stevens and Sons Ltd., 1958.

Aristotle. *Nicomachean Ethics.* Cambridge: Hackett Publishing Co., 1986.

Ayer, A.J. *Truth, Language and Logic.* New York: Dover Publications, 1950.

Barcalow, E. *Moral Philosophy: Theories and Issues.* Belmont: Thomson Wadsworth, 2007.

Beckwith, F.J. *Doing the Right Thing.* Belmont: Thomson Wadsworth, 2002.

Bennaars, G.A. *Ethics, Education and Development.* Nairobi: East African Educational Publishers, 1998.

Bentham, J. *Introduction to the Principles of Morals and Legislation.* New York: Doubleday and Company, Inc., 1961.

Birsh, D. *Ethical Insights: A Brief Introduction.* London: Mayfield Publishing Co., 1998.

Brandt, R.B. *Ethical Theory.* Englewood Cliffs. N.J.: Prentice-Hall, Inc., 1959.

Brandt, R.B (ed.) *Values and Obligation.* New York: Harcourt Brace Jovanovich, Inc., 1961.

Copi, I.M. *Introduction to Logic.* New York: MacMillan, 1982.

Coughlin, G.G. *Your Introduction to Law.* London: Barnes and Nobles Inc., 1971.

Denise, T.C. *Great Traditions in Ethics.* Belmont: Wadsworth Publishing Company, 1992.

Denning, A. *The Road to Justice*. London: Stevens and Sons Ltd., 1955.

Frankena, W.K. *Ethics*. New Delhi: Prentice-Hall of India, 1993.

Garner, R.T. *Moral Philosophy*. New York: The MacMillan Company, 1967.

Gichure, C.W. *Basic Concepts in Ethics*. Nairobi: Focus Books, 1997.

Gonsalves, M.A. *Right and Reason*. London: Charles E. Merrill Publishing Co., 1986.

Harris, C.E. *Applying Moral Theories*. Belmont: Thomson Wadsworth, 2007.

Hausman, A et al. *Logic and Philosophy*. Belmont: Thomson Wadsworth, 2007.

Hobbes, T. *Leviathan*. Middlesex: Penguin Books, 1985.

Hudson, W.D. *Modern Moral Philosophy*. London: The MacMillan Press Ltd., 1978.

Hume, D. *An Enquiry Concerning the Principles of Morals*. Oxford: Clarendon Press, 1894.

Hume, D. *On Human Nature and the Understanding*. New York: The MacMillan Company, 1965.

Hume, D. *Treatise of Human Nature*. New York: Prometheus Books, 1992.

Hurley, P.J. *A Concise Introduction to Logic*. Belmont: Wadsworth Publishing Co., 1991.

Jones, G et al. *Moral Philosophy: A Guide to Ethical Theory*. London: Hodder Murray, 2006.

Kant, I. *Foundations of the Metaphysic of Morals*. New York: The Liberal Arts Press, 1959.

Lillie, W. *An Introduction to Ethics*. New Delhi: Allied Publishers Ltd., 1997.

Mackie, J.L. *Ethics: Inventing Right and Evil*. Middlesex: Penguin Books, 1985.

Martin, M.W. *Everyday Morality: An Introduction to Applied Ethics*. Belmont: Thomson Wadsworth, 2007.

Melden, A.I (ed.) *Ethical Theories*. Englewood Cliffs, N.J.: Prentice-Hall, Inc., 1967.

Mill, J.S. *Utilitarianism, Liberty and Representative Government*. London: J.M. Dent and Sons, 1968.

Moberly, W. *The Ethics of Punishment*. London: Faber and Faber, 1968.

Moore, G.E. *Principia Ethica*. New York: Prometheus Books, 1992.

Murphy, J.D (ed.) *Civil Disobedience and Violence*. Belmont: Wadsworth Publishing Company, Inc., 1971.

Nietzsche, F. *Beyond Good and Evil*. Baltimore: Penguin, 1973.

Ochieng'-Odhiambo, F. *Logic and Induction*. Nairobi: Stantex Publishers, 1996.

Ochieng'-Odhiambo, F. *Introductory Symbolic Logic*. Nairobi: Consolata Institute of Philosophy Press, 2003.

Ochieng'-Odhiambo, F et al (eds.) *Conversations in Philosophy*. Newcastle: Cambridge Scholars Publishing, 2008.

Odera Oruka, H. *Ethics*. Nairobi: Nairobi University Press, 1990.

Odera Oruka, H. *Punishment and Terrorism in Africa*. Nairobi: Kenya Literature Bureau, 1985.

Percesepe, G. (ed.) *Introduction to Ethics*. New Jersey: Prentice-Hall, 1995.

Pojman, L. P. *How Should We Live? An Introduction to Ethics*. Belmont: Thomson Wadsworth, 2005.

Pojman, L.P. *Ethical Theory: Classic and Contemporary Readings*. Belmont: Wadsworth, 2002.

Pojman, L (ed.) *Moral Philosophy: A Reader*. Indianapolis: Hackett Publishing Co., 1993.

Porter, B.F. *The Good Life: Alternative to Ethics*. New York: Ardsley House Publishers, 1995.

Quine, W.V.O. *Methods of Logic*. London: Routledge and Keegan Paul, 1972.

Rafalko, R.J. *Logic for an Overcast Tuesday*. Belmont: Wadsworth Publishing Co., 1991.

Ross, W.D. *Foundations of Ethics*. Oxford: Clarendon Press, 1939.

Ross, W.D. *The Right and the Good.* New York: Oxford University Press, 1930.

Sidgwick, H. *The Methods of Ethics.* New York: Dover Publications, 1966.

Singer, P. (ed.) *Ethics.* Oxford: Oxford University Press, 1994.

Sterba, J.P. *Morality in Practice.* Belmont: Wadsworth Publishing Co., 1991.

Taylor, P.W. (ed.) *Problems of Moral Philosophy.* Belmont: Dickenson Publishing Company, Inc., 1972.

Teichman, J. *Philosophy: A Beginner's Guide.* Oxford: Blackwell, 1988.

Titus, H.H. *Living Issues in Philosophy.* New York: American Book Company, 1964.

Velasquez, M. *Philosophy: A Text with Readings.* Belmont: Thomson Wadsworth, 2008.

Wise, R.L. *Legal Ethics.* New York: Matthew Bender and Co., 1970.

Index

Act-utilitarianism, 47, 183, 185
  definition of, 47
Additive whole, 135
  definition of, 135
Anything that Works, 106
Basic Teleological Principle
  (BTP), 58, 151, 197
  description of, 48
Capital punishment, 130
Concept of justice, 90, 198
  wrong independent of the
    consequences See also
    Wrongness, 198
  wrong no matter what the
    consequences See also
    Wrongness, 198
Cultural relativism, 195
Deontological considerations,
  112
Deontological obligations, 117
Deontological theory of
  punishment, 198, 199
Deontologist, 104, 198
Deontologist and teleologist
  differences, 58
  epistemological differences, 59
Deontologist-retributivist, 199
Deontology, 47, 152, 199
  a problem, 115
  and moral common sense, 117
  and recividism, 199
  deathbed promises, 65, 198
  past looking, 198
  repeat offender, 115
  strengths, 152
  weaknesses, 152
Disagreement
  types of, 38, 196

Dreyfus Affair, 115, 187, 199
  and theoretical dispute, 199
Epistemological circumstances,
  165
Epistemological relativism, 19
Ethical absolutism, 1, 32, 195
  basic principle of universality, 34
Ethical egoism. *See*
  Utilitarianism
Ethical relativism, 1, 195, 196
  definition of, 3
  restricted, 19
  unrestricted, 19
Ethical theories
  types of, 47
Ethical theory
  definition of, 47
Ethical universalism, 47
Ethics
  understanding of, ix
Formalism, 198
  question of justice, 99
Formalist view, 95, 102, 198
Generalisation argument
  and celibacy, 175
  basic structure, 165
  definition of, 153
  epistemological circumstances,
    166
  example of, 153, 178
  exceptions, 176
  reformulation of, 173
Good-indicating characteristics,
  197
Good-making characteristics, 197
Hume, David, 25
  and question of truth, 25
Hybrid judgements, 41

example of, 41
Hybrid judgment, 197
Judgements
   characteristics, 25
   moral, 25
   value, 25
Kant, I., 57
Merits and demerits of payback, 127
Mob justice, 129
Modus tollens, 51, 198
Moore, G. E., 35
   and the concept of 'good', 35
Moral concepts, 8
Moral judgements, 6, 197, 198
Moral principles, 133
   apparent exceptions, 147
   exceptions, 133
      additive whole, 133
Moral theory, 82, 97, 198
Moral view, 71, 97, 198
Natural justice, 127
Negative moral debts or claims, 121
Notion of formalism, 198
Objectively right act, 53, 197
Organic Whole, 138
   genuine exceptions, 138
Pain, and suffering
   general moral statements, 148
Pay-back behaviour, 125
Pleasure and happiness, 142
Positive moral debts or claims, 119
   solicited, 120
   unsolicited, 120
Posteriori, 39
Prima facie, 13
Prima facie and resultant judgements
   distinction of, 30
Prima facie moral judgement

expression of, 30
Principles of belief, 5, 195
Priori, 39
Promising
   Utilitarian theory, 63
Punishment
   retributive view, 147
Recidivism, 104, 199
Reductio ad absurdum, 50
Reinforcement, 107
   negative, 107
   positive, 107
Restricted ethical relativism, 5, 195
Restricted general relativism, 19
Restricted retributivist view, 198
Retributive punishment
   definition of, 125
Retributivist, 104
Retributivist theory of punishment, 126
Rule-utilitarianism, 47, 107, 183, 192
   an alternative to utilitarianism-deontology, 183
Subjectively right act, 197
Subjectivity problem, 197
Supervenience, 7, 25
   and universality, 160
Supervenience and universality, 30
Teleological principle, 163
Terms of fairness, 164
Thought-experiment, 135
Torts, 118
Truths
   a posteriori, 25
   a priori, 25
   analytic, 26
   contingent, 26
   necessary, 26
Undesirable consequences, 164

Universality, 25
Unrestricted ethical relativism, 195
Unrestricted general relativism, 19
Unrestricted retributivist view, 198
Utilitarian
 and keeping of promises, 55
 and preventive crime, 107
 and subjectivity problem, 50
 and theory of punishment, 107
Utilitarian promise, 69
Utilitarian theory of punishment, 198
Utilitarian view, 198

Utilitarianism, 47, 151, 197, 199, *See also* ethical universalism
 and preventive punishment, 107
 and promises, 190, 199
 as an ethical theory, 56
 future looking, 198
 languages, 190, 199
 public disclosure, 94, 199
 strengths, 151
 weaknesses, 151
Value relativism, 31
Wrongness
 independent of consequences *See also* Concept of justice, 198
 no matter what the consequences, 198

www.ingramcontent.com/pod-product-compliance
Lightning Source LLC
Chambersburg PA
CBHW031550300426
44111CB00006BA/250